MITZVAH

The *Basic Jewish Ideas* Series

MITZVAH

JACOB NEUSNER

Chappaqua, NY

LC 81–22705
ISBN 0–940646–25–0
First Edition

*Cover photos courtesy of the National
Aeronautics and Space Administration.*

Acknowledgments

Professor David Altshuler, George Washington University, did two important jobs with this book. First, he edited the manuscript as I wrote it, and he gave me important and valuable criticism. Second, he took complete charge of the Hebrew texts, setting them forth and translating them—in all ways preparing the Hebrew parts of this book. I am very grateful to him both for his editorial help and for his taking an important share of readying the book for the printer.

My wife, Suzanne Richter Neusner, drew the designs that appear in this book.

In memory of
Jason D. Frerichs
1978–1981

CONTENTS

MITZVAH

YOU ARE GOING TO BECOME COMMANDED

If you are approaching the age of thirteen, you find yourself changing. The changes come in many ways. Some are physical, changes in your body as you near, reach, or pass puberty. Others take place inside you, changes in how you see or feel or think about things. At just this time in your life, your family and synagogue celebrate these changes in you. The celebration is your *bar mitzvah* or *bat mitzvah*. On this occasion, people recognize that these changes are important. They show they are glad and proud to see them happen.

At this same time, your family and the community of Israel, the Jewish people, of which you are part, say something about these changes. They say what they think these changes *should* mean.

The message adds up to one thing: you are beginning to be responsible for yourself and for what you do. You are not yet an adult. But you are no longer a child. You enter a shadow world, a gray place. You are no longer what you were. You are not yet what you will be. But all eyes are on your future—and so, too, are all the bets.

How does the community of Israel, the Jewish people, recognize and celebrate these wonderful changes of body and soul that come upon you? They declare that you are now *commanded*. That is, you are recognized as a *bar mitzvah* or a *bat mitzvah*, a person subject to a mitzvah. Surely this, too, is some kind of change. But what kind? What difference is there between someone who is commanded and someone who is not commanded?

Becoming Commanded

The place to begin answering is in the meaning of your *becoming* commanded. You are nearing the "age of commandments," that is, the age of bar mitzvah or bat mitzvah. You know that *mitzvah* means commandment. Some people think that bar mitzvah or bat mitzvah should be translated as "son" or "daughter" of a commandment. That is what the words say: *bar* is Hebrew for "son" and *bat* is Hebrew for "daughter." But that is not what the words mean. "Son" or "daughter" here means "subject to." You are becoming "subject to" the commandments, responsible for carrying them out.

This change fits in with the other changes taking place in you. These days you have begun to think about things in new ways. Before, someone else decided. You did what others said. You lived in a world made up of school, home, family, friends. Now you know that there is a world beyond that world, a strange place, a place of challenge and excitement. Perhaps you have begun to do things by yourself—things that, in the past, others did for you or you had to do with others.

When you were very young, you learned how to cross the street by yourself. And you did cross the street by yourself. That was one step toward becoming responsible for yourself. Since then you have taken many other steps. The one in front of you is a giant step: a step outward toward the world, away from only school, only home, only family, only friends. Something more is coming.

What is this something more? It is the discovery that there is a you apart from home, school, friends, family. It is a you that decides things. It is a you that has opinions not given to you by others. It is a you that has preferences. You have begun to say what you think, what you want. You are becoming a person in your own right. Certainly, you can remember when you wanted whatever your parents wanted (or, sometimes, the very opposite). Now you can think of things that you want no matter what anyone else wants or does not want. That is what I mean by something more. It is a you beyond anyone who makes you or tells you what to do or what to be.

Now the discovery of this you may sometimes lead you to want to be by yourself, to daydream, to think your own thoughts. At times you may consider what you will be in the future—an architect, or a doctor, or a star in the Olympics, or president. In these thoughts a new person is being born, a you beyond the you made by the world around you. For a long time, the world told you who you are. Now you want to tell the world who you are. That is how it should be.

Who Am I? You Should Be. . .

This is on your mind: Who am I? What am I going to be? Who am I now that I am becoming someone?

What is coming to you, quite simply, is a set of answers to this question: *This* is what you should be. *This* is what you should do.

The word "command" hardly needs to be defined. It is a statement of something you must do, something that you must do because the one who wants you to do it has the say-so to tell you to do it.

When your father or your mother tells you to do something, it may be good advice, such as "Don't eat junk food." Or it may be a command, such as "Do this. Period." or "Don't dare do that." A commandment, when it is a mitzvah, is what God tells us to do or not to do. It is what God tells all of us in general and what God tells each of us in particular.

What a conflict! On the one side you are emerging from the childhood of parents' advice and commandments. All your years people have been telling you what to do. Now you are becoming something more than a child (a "teenager"), and just as you pass from one point in life to the next, what happens? You move from your parents' commandments and become—what? A bar mitzvah, a bat mitzvah, a person subject to and responsible for God's commandments. Have you just exchanged one boss for another?

That is the issue of becoming commanded. You are now free to become yourself. And, in our community as Jews, that means to become what we are commanded to be. It seems a heavy and difficult thing. Even the idea of it has to be unpacked and repacked, taken apart and put back together again, so we can make sense of it all.

Let's not talk about the world in general—what I think or what someone else thinks. We are going to talk about a very specific corner of the world, the Jewish corner. We are not talking about a celebration of becoming a teenager or of puberty, in general; but the specific Jewish celebration called bar or bat mitzvah. We are Jews talking about Judaism. To use Jewish language, we are "Israel," the Jewish people; and we are "studying Torah." So I am not going to tell you what I personally think. You need not pay attention to me. I am going to tell you a few things that the greatest rabbis, teachers, of Israel, the Jewish people, have had to say about mitzvah.

You and Israel, You and Torah

When you go to the Holy Ark and take the Torah and read it for the community, when you chant a prophetic passage, when you lead the community in prayer, you are not doing it all by and for yourself. You do it because you are becoming part of the community. You are taking your place in the community. You are becoming one of "Israel," the Jewish people. So part of your task is to discover what that has meant to Jews before us. And part of it is to take up being commanded. You must discover what that can mean for you.

Still, you cannot make up Judaism every day when you get up in the morning, any more than you can invent the wheel. It is there. You also cannot take over Judaism as someone else has made it for you. Without discovering the place and the part waiting for you in that Judaism, there is no you. True, out there is a life of Torah and commandments, beginning with the celebration of your approaching manhood or womanhood. But in here is your life being celebrated.

These two, then—you and Torah—come together. That is what is celebrated. That is why your place, your part, the discovery of you—these are the occasion. Without you there would be no celebration. Without the Torah there would be nothing to celebrate.

Do You Want to Be Commanded?

In the excitement of becoming a bat or bar mitzvah, you must not allow yourself to be hustled into something you have not accepted. I realize that it is unthinkable, at this time in your life, to say, But what if I do not wish to be commanded? Do I have a choice in the matter? Is this how things must be?

What will it mean to you to become subject to the commandments? It will mean that you take on ways of living, ways of thinking, ways of seeing the world, that come to you and to all Israel, the Jewish people, from God. It will mean that things you have done because your family did them, or because your synagogue or temple did them, or because your rabbi said to do them, now have to be done because you, personally, individually, are responsible to do them—because you are a part of Israel. It is a change in life, not because the day after you celebrate reaching the age of *mitzvot* (your bar mitzvah or bat mitzvah) you say, "Today I shall do this." Today you may do what you did yesterday. But you do it in a different setting.

There are no simple examples, but examples are all we have. Let us say that you go out for the track team in your school, or the swimming team. The day before you make the team, you run a mile or swim a half-mile. The day after you make the team, you run a mile or swim a half-mile. What has changed? Only this: on the day you made the team the coach told you to run or swim. The next day you do it not merely because you feel like it, but because now you are responsible to run or swim—it is now part of the definition of you as a person.

What happens if you do not want to do the running or swimming? You don't do it. What follows? You are not on the team.

Are you free to choose? You certainly are. But before, if you did not run or swim there were no consequences. Now, there are. Before, you might have been an excellent runner or swimmer, but now your running and swimming have a different meaning. You chose to be on the team; now you have a responsibility to the team. Now the coach cares, the team cares.

Now you are important because the whole community of Israel, the Jewish people, care that you do what you are supposed to do.

What if You Don't Want to Become a Bat or Bar Mitzvah?

Clearly, you have many things to decide now that you have become responsible for your decisions. The main one is this: Do you wish to accept the responsibilities of being a bat or bar mitzvah? Anyone who thinks you do not have that choice simply is wrong. And even if you go through the parties and the public celebration, even if you are called to the Torah and say the blessings and read what you are taught to read—you still have to make that choice.

Let us say that you choose not to become a bar or bat mitzvah. You go through the ceremony—but that is all it is to you: a ceremony, not a celebration, not a turning. What difference does it make?

If you do not join the swimming team, the team will still compete; and if you do not join the track team, it will still represent your school. Israel, the Jewish people, lives forever. God brought the Jewish people, Israel, into being. We shall be here until the end of time. I won't, and you won't, but Israel will. So do not think that if you choose not to become responsible for the mitzvot, the mitzvot will cease to be. Do not think that if you choose to leave the synagogue and community of Israel, they will go away. They will be there, but you won't.

That is the difference. It all depends on you, because now for the first time in your life, you are responsible for yourself. You decide what happens to you in ways you never have before. Just as you grow to bodily maturity, so too you grow toward maturity as a citizen of Israel, the Jewish people.

So reaching the age of mitzvot, becoming a bat or bar mitzvah, is a time of choice. The choice is not whether or not you will choose to obey. By that I mean, do what you do because you are commanded, not merely because you feel like it.

LOOKING BACK, LOOKING FORWARD

These are the main points in this chapter: (1) You are now changing in your body and in your mind. The community of Israel, the Jewish people, celebrates these changes because they mark your reaching the age of mitzvot. (2) The age of mitzvot is the age at which you become commanded. (3) There is a likeness between the changes in your self and the changes in your position in the Jewish community. Just as you are becoming a person on your own, so you are received as a person on your own. (4) When you reach the age of commandments, become bat or bar mitzvah, you reflect on who you are and what you want to be. The commandments turn good advice into responsibilities. (5) The commandments are the "can" and "should" of our lives. To be commanded is to be and do what God wants us to be and do. (6) You have a choice to obey or not. When you choose to be commanded, that is, to accept your responsibilities as a Jew, you do things you did before. But now you do them because you are responsible to do them. (7) But you have the right not to become commanded; and you have the duty, as you approach your bar or bat mitzvah, to exercise the right of choice.

Now we have to ask, What difference does it make if you choose to be commanded? What is the meaning of being commanded? What are the changes? These are the questions of the next chapter.

NOT ONLY WHAT TO DO BUT ESPECIALLY WHY TO DO IT

One of the great rabbis of the Talmud made a statement that tells us the entire message of what it means to be commanded: "Greater is the one who is commanded and does something, than the one who is not commanded and does it." The whole story is in that one sentence. To put it in its simplest form: *A person who does something but is not commanded to do it is different from a person who does something and is commanded to do it.* Doing it because you feel like it and doing it because you are commanded are not the same.

Let's unpack that sentence.

(A) The "something" is one and the same thing. What makes a mitzvah into a mitzvah is not that it is different—a different action, a different feeling, something out of the ordinary. Two people may be doing the same thing and for only one of them is it a mitzvah.

(B) What you do may or may not be a mitzvah depending on what you are thinking or feeling or hoping or intending when you do it.

(C) One more thing to consider is the circumstance. *Why* and *for what* are joined by *when*.

Here is a case: You light a candle. It may be a candle on a birthday cake. It may be a candle you light during a power failure. It may be a candle at sunset on the evening before the Sabbath.

The first candle celebrates. It is meant to be blown out. The second candle illuminates. It is meant to be used. The third candle consecrates, makes holy. It is meant to be appreciated, to burn, yet not to be used for any other purpose.

Everything depends on your purpose and the circumstance. The candle may be one and the same. But the time is not. Or the occasion is not. Or your own motive or reason for lighting it is not.

So lighting a candle may or may not be a mitzvah. What you say when you light the candle—"Happy birthday," or "The lights just went out," or ". . . who has sanctified us by the commandments and commanded us to light the Sabbath light"—that makes all the difference.

Being commanded means having the power to make the difference. If you do things merely because you

The Teaching

From the Talmud: Kiddushin 30a

גָּדוֹל מְצֻוֶּה וְעוֹשֶׂה מִמִּי שֶׁאֵינוֹ מְצֻוֶּה וְעוֹשֶׂה.

Greater is the one who is commanded and does something, than the one who is not commanded and does it.

feel like doing them, because they are nice or feel good or make sense, then, so far as the third of the three candles goes, it is not a mitzvah. Only if you are commanded can you make a candle into a Sabbath candle. Only if you are a bar mitzvah or a bat mitzvah can you turn lighting the candle into: " . . . who has sanctified us . . . "

Now that you are becoming a bar mitzvah or a bat mitzvah, you are growing into that power. Up until now you have not had it.

Let's go more deeply into these ideas since they are the key to understanding what is before us: the idea of being commanded, and what the idea of being commanded means to you.

Becoming a bar or bat mitzvah involves partners: first of all, you; second of all, the Jewish people, Israel, which you now join.

There is a change going on in you as a person, in your body and in your self; and that change is what marks a change in you as a Jew, in your place in the Jewish people and in your responsibilities—the things you may do, the things you now must do. If you understand mitzvah and what it means, you can and will relate the changes in yourself to the changes in your standing. Then becoming a bat mitzvah or a bar mitzvah can do more than mark or celebrate a change in your life. It can really change your life. You can change your life through becoming a real bar or bat mitzvah!

The Jewish Community Sees You Differently

There is also a change in the Jewish community, in the synagogue. The community wants and needs you. Everybody celebrates because everybody looks forward to your being a responsible citizen. Jews love and respect the Jewish people, one by one. Every Jew is precious. Each Jew can have the power to make something holy. And that changes the community.

A sign of that change—and of the fact that you now count—is that you are now numbered as a part of a *minyan*, the quorum of three people to say Grace after Meals, or ten people to pray as a community. The community knows that you now have the power in your mind and heart to make things holy, to turn an ordinary action into a mitzvah. To enter the community, to take your place within Israel, is to share in the strength and power of the community to turn the lighting of a candle into the sanctification of the Sabbath day.

Bending Your Will

But sharing, as we are about to see in the next example, may not always be easy. There may be times when we must bend our will and power to the needs of the community; and times when the community bends its will and power to do a mitzvah just because it is commanded. In looking at what a great rabbi of ancient times says, we want to hear him speak in the terms he thinks are important. Then we shall translate what he says into terms we think are important.

> *Rabbi Eleazar ben Azariah says, How do we prove from Scripture that a person should not say, "I do not want to eat pork [or do other forbidden things]," rather a person should say, "I do want to eat pork. But what can I do? For my heavenly parent has commanded me not to do it."*
>
> *From the following verse of Scripture we prove that fact: And I have separated you from the peoples, that you should be mine.*
>
> *When a person becomes separate from sin and takes up the yoke of Heaven,* [then that person becomes Mine].

One of the differences which we in North America and Great Britain have learned to respect is the fact that many good Jews do not observe the Jewish dietary laws, a fact that does not keep them from being good Jews in any large sense. So the purpose of quoting this saying of Eleazar ben Azariah is not to tell those who do not keep the Jewish dietary laws that they are sinning. It is to stress Eleazar's attitude. Doing the mitzvot is not a matter of

The Teaching

From Sifra: Kedoshim 11:22

ר׳ אֶלְעָזָר בֶּן עֲזַרְיָה אוֹמֵר,
מְנַיִן שֶׁלֹּא יֹאמַר אָדָם ...
אִי אִפְשִׁי לֶאֱכֹל בְּשַׂר
חֲזִיר ... אֲבָל אִיפְשִׁי מָה
אֶעֱשֶׂה וְאָבִי שֶׁבַּשָּׁמַיִם גָּזַר
עָלַי כָּךְ.

תַּלְמוּד לוֹמַר: וָאַבְדִּיל
אֶתְכֶם מִן הָעַמִּים לִהְיוֹת
לִי.

נִמְצָא פּוּרֵשׁ מִן הָעֲבֵירָה
וּמְקַבֵּל עָלָיו מַלְכוּת
שָׁמַיִם.

Rabbi Eleazar ben Azariah says, How do we prove from Scripture that a person should not say, "I do not want to eat pork [or do other forbidden things]," rather a person should say, "I do want to eat pork. But what can I do? For my heavenly Parent has commanded me not to do it."

From the following verse of Scripture we prove that fact: *And I have separated you from the peoples, that you should be Mine* (Leviticus 20:26).

When a person becomes separate from sin and takes up the yoke of Heaven, [then that person becomes Mine].

how we feel, what we like or do not like. It may well be a matter of how we do *not* feel. He uses the example of pork because, in his time, it was simple and convenient—something shared by all Jews. We shall point to other examples that are similarly shared in our own time.

The important thing is that you know you are commanded; that there are things God wants from you. You are important. Whether what God wants has to do with one thing or some other must be settled within your synagogue or temple, within your home and family.

Let's proceed to what Eleazar is saying. It is really very straightforward. What we do or avoid doing may or may not be a mitzvah. It depends upon whether we have used our inner power to turn our action into a mitzvah.

We use the example of not eating certain foods, as Eleazar did, because that is easy to understand. Perhaps you do not happen to care for brussels sprouts or liver. To some people, myself included, that comes naturally. Your feelings or reasons for leaving brussels sprouts and liver—and sometimes even pork—on your plate may have nothing at all to do with yourself in the sight of God and of the people of Israel.

Perhaps, however, you find a wallet that belongs to someone else. Her name is in it; and all the same, you really want to keep it. Or perhaps you *do* want to hurt someone else's feelings. But you do not do these things. You avoid doing them not only one time or two times. You never do them. Why not?

Because, as Jews traditionally believe, God has told Israel that there are some things Jews do not do. They do not hurt other people. They do not hesitate to return lost property when once they know who lost it.

There is nothing just plain natural, or simply human, about obeying these rules. There is nothing normal or everyday in giving up what you want to keep or not doing what you want to do. But you decide, by choosing, why you do one thing and why you do not do something else—and that makes all the difference. The reason is mitzvah: commandment.

If you are commanded to do something, or if you are commanded and so do not do something, then you are a bar mitzvah or bat mitzvah. Then you have the power, which otherwise you do not have, to turn what is ordinary and routine into something extraordinary and holy.

The Ordinary

You know that Jews live common lives, lives just like their neighbors live. They work, they rest, they eat and sleep. So when we speak about commandments, we do not talk especially about doing things that are uncommon. Some commandments speak about what we do and do not do on a special day like the Sabbath. Other commandments tell us about foods we eat or do not eat. Still others, the most important ones, speak about what we do with other people and how we feel toward other people. There is nothing unnatural or odd in all these things to which the commandments speak. On the contrary, to be commanded is to do what everyone does—but in a special way.

The day you become commanded, you are the same person you were the day before. The morning after, you will do pretty much the same things you have always done. Then what changes?

As we have said, what changes is *why* you do things one way and not some other. Let's take two simple examples, one dealing with the holy and one with the ordinary.

Let us take the matter of the Sabbath or going to synagogue services. You may not do on the Sabbath what you do on ordinary days, and so you may be a Sabbath-observer. You may go to a synagogue on the Sabbath. If you did the week before your bar or bat mitzvah, before you became commanded, you did it because you felt like it, or because someone else wanted you to. But once you are a bar or bat mitzvah, you will do it for a new reason. It will be because Jews are commanded to keep the Sabbath, not because you merely feel like doing it.

Let us take something that seems ordinary but is equally important. Someone in school has misplaced or lost a book. You find the book. You figure out who owns it. You bring the book back to that person. Now if you did that the day before your bat or bar mitzvah, before you became commanded, you did it because you felt like it or thought it was right or because you would feel like a good person if you did it. But once you are commanded you do it for a different reason. You do it because Jews are supposed to do it. You do it because you are commanded to do it, because being honest and returning someone's lost property is a mitzvah.

To be commanded is a change that takes place within. It is a way of looking at the ordinary world and seeing everything in it that can be made holy. It is the holy way of life we call Judaism.

LOOKING BACK, LOOKING FORWARD

These are the main points in this chapter: (1) To be commanded is not to do something new, but to do something you may already do—for a different reason. (2) A mitzvah is something you do whether or not you feel like doing it—because God wants you to do so, because you are commanded. (3) The power to turn a deed into a mitzvah is within you, in your attitudes and feelings. (4) The changes you feel and the changes in the community's attitude toward you both celebrate the power you gain, as a bar or bat mitzvah, to turn an ordinary deed into a mitzvah. That is the main thing that happens to you when you reach the age of mitzvot. (5) When you reach the age of mitzvot, how you feel and what you think matter. Then you become commanded and you gain the power to do something because you are commanded. (6) The power to do something because it is a mitzvah is the power to make something ordinary into something holy.

The logical next step is to find out what the mitzvot are. Since tradition tells us that God gave the commandments in the Torah, the answer should be obvious. Look into the Torah and make a list. Then you know the commandments. But that is not so easy. There are a great many mitzvot in the Torah. Some of them are large and general. Others are very concrete and specific. Many of them apply to worlds other than the world we live in. So we have to sort them out. Above all, some commandments obviously are going to be more important than others. So we need advice on which ones count more than others. That is what the next chapter tells us.

WHAT ARE MITZVOT?

You may have heard that something is a mitzvah. In everyday conversation, people often say this to mean that doing a certain deed is a good thing. Up to now we have said that a mitzvah is an ordinary deed you do, or do not do. And that your attitude in doing it or not doing it is what makes it into a mitzvah. Now you must have an urgent question. Is a mitzvah just anything? Or are there some things that are really mitzvot, and other things that cannot be mitzvot? How many possible mitzvot are there? And how do I count them? What do they all mean?

Our job in this chapter is to sort out these questions and show how the great minds of the Jewish heritage answer them.

The Problem

The prophets of the Bible and the rabbis of the Talmud faced a problem. Even though these two groups of Jewish masters lived many years apart in terms of time, the problem was the same one. When you look through the books of Torah, you will see the problem for yourself. There are many commandments of various kinds in the Five Books of Moses. Some of them tell us what to do or not to do in the Temple. Some of them speak of things that mattered in ancient times alone, or only to life in the Holy Land, the Land of Israel. But many of the commandments apply to the lives of Jews wherever and whenever they live. So the rabbis of the Talmud asked whether there were some few basic commandments to keep in mind, and they also wanted to know whether some commandments are more important than others. But do not think they were trying to simplify anything.

The Whole Torah—All the Commandments

Let us start with a very famous saying. It is placed into the setting of a story. Someone comes before a great rabbi and asks him to state what Judaism is all about, very briefly. The request is dramatic: "Tell me the entire Torah while you are standing on one foot." Hillel, who lived two thousand years ago, did not regard the man's question as rude or foolish. He answered it so well, the Talmud tells us, that the man, a non-Jew, converted to Judaism. Here is Hillel's answer:

What is hateful to yourself do not do to your neighbor.
That is the whole Torah. All the rest is commentary.
Now go and study.

Hillel does not talk of the mitzvot directly. But what he says tells us what mitzvot he thought most important. They are the ones that tell us how to act with other people. In defining Judaism, Hillel also defines the important commandments.

That's a good start, but let's look deeper. Hillel was neither the first nor the last to try to give a short definition of Judaism. He chose four parts for his definition: (1) He selected, from among many wonderful passages of Torah, the verse from Leviticus 19:18, "You shall love your neighbor as yourself: I am the Lord." This commandment, Hillel believed, summarized everything. (2) He spoke of Torah. He did not speak of "Judaism," but of Torah. (3) He spoke of everything else in the tradition as "commentary"—that is, as examples of this single principle. (4) Last, he told the man to go, not to the synagogue for prayer or to the Temple for sacrifice; not to those who taught meditation or to the bands of zealots preparing for a holy war to bring the days of the messiah closer; but to the schoolhouse for study of Torah.

So, for Hillel the important mitzvot are the ones that detail how we act toward other people.

You Were Made to Learn Torah

One generation later another great teacher, who carried on the tradition of Hillel, said what he thought the main

The Teaching

From the Talmud: Shabbat 31a

דַּעֲלָךְ סְנֵי לְחַבְרָךְ לָא
תַּעֲבֵיד זוֹ הִיא כָּל הַתּוֹרָה
כּוּלָהּ, וְאִידָךְ — פֵּירוּשָׁהּ
הוּא, זִיל גְּמוֹר.

What is hateful to yourself do not do to your neighbor. That is the whole Torah. All the rest is commentary. Now go and study.

commandment was. He took a different line of thought. He wanted to know why the people of Israel are here on earth, what the purpose of living is. So when he speaks of the most important thing we can do, he asks about why it is important that we live and breathe. This is what Hillel's great student, Yohanan ben Zakkai, taught:

> *If you have done much in study of Torah, do not take credit for yourself, because you were created for this purpose.*

In other words, our whole reason for being is to study Torah—that is, revelation. Here, too, no one speaks of mitzvah. Yet from what Yohanan ben Zakkai says, we know what mitzvah he will regard as most important. It is the mitzvah of studying Torah, since Torah reveals mitzvot.

The Teaching

From the Mishnah: Avot 2:8

אִם לָמַדְתָּ תּוֹרָה הַרְבֵּה,
אַל תַּחֲזִיק טוֹבָה לְעַצְמֶךָ,
כִּי לְכַךְ נוֹצָרְתָּ.

If you have done much in study of Torah, do not take credit for yourself, because you were created for this purpose.

Before moving on, think for a moment about this mitzvah. How do you study Torah? Why do you do it?

What you do, the action you follow, may simply be to read a book. Or you may engage in a discussion about a teaching in the Torah or in the Mishnah or in some other holy book of Judaism. Now, is that studying Torah? It *may* be, but not always.

You can read a book for a number of different reasons. You may want the information in that book. You may want to know facts. Is that studying Torah? No. There is a difference between seeking facts and ideas (studying) and seeking revelation (performing the mitzvah of "studying Torah"). Once again, it is your attitude that makes the difference. When you study Torah you seek revelation, you want to know what God and God's prophets and sages want to tell you.

On the one hand, you may study Scriptures or the Mishnah or the Prayer Book merely to find out what is in these books. You go through the books. On the other hand, you may study Scriptures or Mishnah or the Prayer Book to find out what in those books should enter into your very life. The books go through you. They change you. They change you because you want to be shaped and formed by them.

So the principal mitzvah, Yohanan ben Zakkai says, is to study Torah. And that means that he wants you to be changed by the Torah. You do not go through the Torah. The Torah goes through you.

When you take up a Jewish book because you see yourself as commanded to do so, then you carry out the mitzvah of studying Torah. Then it is no longer an ordinary book. It is Torah, and you need to learn it.

Only 613 Mitzvot!

Hillel's statement and Yohanan's teaching leave us wondering about all the other mitzvot. If all we need are a few basic ones, why are there so many? This is especially puzzling if you happen to know the number 613.

Why 613? Because in many places you will read or hear that, in all, there are precisely 613 commandments, no more and no fewer. Many books have been written in which people lovingly counted up the commandments to reach the figure 613. Some people have seen the need to ask why there are not 614 or 612 or 903 or any other number. So, if you have heard the number 613 you must wonder what that number means (and how Hillel and Yohanan ben Zakkai forgot to mention it).

In fact, the number 613 is made up of two other numbers:

> 365—the number of days in the solar year; and
> +248—the number of bones in the body (as counted in ancient times).
>
> 613—the number of commandments

What we have is a very poetic idea. There is a commandment for each day: just as the sun rises and sets, so each day is marked out by a commandment of its own. And there is a commandment for each bone of the body: all of our bones, all of our being, have commandments to do.

Now if you want to ruin the poem being conveyed by the number 613, just ask what your shoulder blade can do. If you want to appreciate the poem, you ask what the poet is trying to say. You would answer this way. The world of nature, represented by sunrise and sunset, and the world of mortal people, represented by their very bones—both worlds, natural and human, are subject to commandments.

You might also discover a further lesson in the poem. Just as the sun reliably does what it is commanded to do, setting in the evening, rising in the morning, so do we do reliably and faithfully what we are commanded to do.

The number, 613 commandments, can be divided in another way. It is the starting point for another definition of the commandments. This one is made up by quoting verses from Scripture. In this definition, prophets and psalmists are asked to explain to us how all of the commandments can be packed up in only a few, or even in one, really basic commandment.

Only One Mitzvah?

This long passage shows how the work is done. It is recorded in the name of Rabbi Simlai.

> *Six hundred and thirteen commandments were given to Moses, three hundred and sixty-five negative ones, corresponding to the number of the days of the solar year, and two hundred forty-eight positive commandments, corresponding to the parts of the human body.*
>
> *David came and reduced them to eleven:* A Psalm of David. Lord, who shall sojourn in your tabernacle, and who shall dwell in your holy mountain? *(1)* The person who walks uprightly and *(2)* works righteousness and *(3)* speaks truth in his heart and *(4)* has no slander on his tongue and *(5)* does no evil to others and *(6)* does not take up a reproach against a neighbor, *(7)* in whose eyes a vile person is despised, but *(8)* honors those who fear the Lord. *(9)* He is truthful even when it may hurt him and changes not [the truth]. *(10)* He does not take a bribe against the innocent.
>
> *Isaiah came and reduced them to six:*
> *(1)* He who walks righteously and *(2)* speaks uprightly, *(3)* who despises the gain of oppressions, *(4)* shakes his hand from holding bribes, *(5)* stops his ear from hearing of

blood, *(6)* and shuts his eyes from looking upon evil, he shall dwell on high.

Micah came and reduced them to three:
It has been told you, man, what is good, and what the Lord demands from you, only *(1)* to do justly, and *(2)* to love mercy, and *(3)* to walk humbly before God.

Isaiah again came and reduced them to two:
Thus says the Lord, *(1)* Keep justice and *(2)* do righteousness.

Amos came and reduced them to a single one, as it is said, For thus says the Lord to the house of Israel. Seek Me and live.

Habakkuk [further] came and based them on one, as it is said, But the righteous shall live by his faith.

This teaching from the Talmud tells us most everything we need to know about the nature of mitzvot.

First, there is special importance placed on the Torah as the source of commandments. The Scriptures are quoted in a creative way—a piece from a prophet here, a piece from a psalmist there—to tell us that we are learning something in the way the rabbi wants to teach it, and from the very source that the rabbi himself learned it.

Second, the rabbi begins the work of defining mitzvot by telling us that there are two kinds. Some mitzvot tell us what we are to do (postive commandments); and some tell us what we are not to do (negative commandments). Judaism is concerned, then, with how we behave, how we conduct our lives.

Third, all the pieces have one thing in common: they all stress the mitzvot that tell us how to behave

The Teaching

שֵׁשׁ מֵאוֹת וּשְׁלֹשׁ עֶשְׂרֵה
מִצְוֹת נֶאֶמְרוּ לוֹ לְמֹשֶׁה,
שְׁלֹשׁ מֵאוֹת וְשִׁשִּׁים וְחָמֵשׁ
לָאוִין כְּמִנְיַן יְמוֹת הַחַמָּה,
וּמָאתַיִם וְאַרְבָּעִים וּשְׁמוֹנָה
עֲשֵׂה כְּנֶגֶד אֵיבָרָיו שֶׁל אָדָם.

בָּא דָוִד וְהֶאֱמִידָן עַל
אַחַת עֶשְׂרֵה, דִּכְתִיב:
מִזְמוֹר לְדָוִד   יְהֹוָה מִי-
יָגוּר בְּאָהֳלֶךְ מִי-יִשְׁכֹּן בְּהַר
קָדְשֶׁךָ. הוֹלֵךְ תָּמִים וּפֹעֵל
צֶדֶק וְדֹבֵר אֱמֶת בִּלְבָבוֹ.
לֹא-רָגַל עַל-לְשֹׁנוֹ לֹא-
עָשָׂה לְרֵעֵהוּ רָעָה וְחֶרְפָּה
לֹא-נָשָׂא עַל-קְרֹבוֹ. נִבְזֶה
בְּעֵינָיו נִמְאָס וְאֶת-יִרְאֵי
יְהֹוָה יְכַבֵּד נִשְׁבַּע לְהָרַע
וְלֹא יָמִר. כַּסְפּוֹ לֹא-נָתַן
בְּנֶשֶׁךְ וְשֹׁחַד עַל-נָקִי לֹא
לָקָח ...

Six hundred and thirteen commandments were given to Moses, three hundred and sixty-five negative ones, corresponding to the number of days of the solar year, and two hundred forty-eight positive commandments, corresponding to the parts of the human body.

David came and reduced them to eleven: *A Psalm of David* (Psalm 15). *Lord, who shall sojourn in Your tabernacle, and who shall dwell in Your holy mountain?* (1) *The person who walks uprightly and* (2) *works righteousness and* (3) *speaks truth in his heart and* (4) *has no slander on his tongue and* (5) *does no evil to others and* (6) *does not take up a reproach against a neighbor,* (7) *in whose eyes a vile person is despised, but* (8) *honors those who fear the Lord.* (9) *He is truthful even when it may hurt him and changes not [the truth].* (10) *He does not take a bribe against the innocent.*

From the Talmud: Makkot 23b–24a

בָּא יְשַׁעְיָהוּ וְהֶעֱמִידָן עַל
שֵׁשׁ, דִּכְתִיב: הֹלֵךְ צְדָקוֹת
וְדֹבֵר מֵישָׁרִים מֹאֵס בְּבֶצַע
מַעֲשַׁקּוֹת נֹעֵר כַּפָּיו מִתְּמֹךְ
בַּשֹּׁחַד אֹטֵם אָזְנוֹ מִשְּׁמֹעַ
דָּמִים וְעֹצֵם עֵינָיו מֵרְאוֹת
בְּרָע. הוּא מְרוֹמִים יִשְׁכֹּן ...
בָּא מִיכָה וְהֶעֱמִידָן עַל
שָׁלוֹשׁ, דִּכְתִיב: הִגִּיד לְךָ
אָדָם מַה־טּוֹב וּמָה־יְהוָה
דּוֹרֵשׁ מִמְּךָ כִּי אִם־עֲשׂוֹת
מִשְׁפָּט וְאַהֲבַת חֶסֶד וְהַצְנֵעַ
לֶכֶת עִם־אֱלֹהֶיךָ.
חָזַר יְשַׁעְיָהוּ וְהֶעֱמִידָן
עַל שְׁתַּיִם, שֶׁנֶּאֱמַר: כֹּה
אָמַר יְהוָה שִׁמְרוּ מִשְׁפָּט
וַעֲשׂוּ צְדָקָה ...
בָּא עָמוֹס וְהֶעֱמִידָן עַל
אַחַת, שֶׁנֶּאֱמַר: כִּי כֹה אָמַר
יְהוָה לְבֵית יִשְׂרָאֵל
דִּרְשׁוּנִי וִחְיוּ.
בָּא חֲבַקּוּק וְהֶעֱמִידָן עַל
אַחַת, שֶׁנֶּאֱמַר: וְצַדִּיק
בֶּאֱמוּנָתוֹ יִחְיֶה.

Isaiah came and reduced them to six (Isaiah 33:15–16): (1) *He who walks righteously and* (2) *speaks uprightly,* (3) *who despises the gain of oppressions,* (4) *shakes his hand from holding bribes,* (5) *stops his ear from hearing of blood,* (6) *and shuts his eyes from looking upon evil, he shall dwell on high.*

Micah came and reduced them to three (Micah 6:8): *It has been told you, man, what is good, and what the Lord demands from you, only* (1) *to do justly, and* (2) *to love mercy, and* (3) *to walk humbly before God.*

Isaiah again came and reduced them to two (Isaiah 56:1): *Thus says the Lord,* (1) *Keep justice and* (2) *do righteousness.*

Amos came and reduced them to a single one, as it is said (Amos 5:4), *For thus says the Lord to the house of Israel. Seek Me and live.*

Habakkuk [further] came and based them on one, as it is said (Habakkuk 2:4), *But the righteous shall live by his faith.*

toward others or how to behave with respect. These ethical and moral mitzvot are the most important. Torah, you remember, means revelation. And, according to the rabbis, what was in fact revealed were mostly ethical teachings. And the rabbis teach us that the *way* of ethics is the search for God. Living a good life means searching for God—*The righteous shall live by his faith*—for, in Hebrew, the word faith is *emunah*, meaning trust, loyalty, commitment. So, we learn that what keeps a person alive, what makes life real and meaningful, is trust in and loyalty to God.

LOOKING BACK, LOOKING FORWARD

These are the main points in this chapter: (1) Hillel said: the important mitzvah is to love one's neighbor as oneself. (2) Yohanan ben Zakkai said: the important mitzvah is to do what comes naturally, which is to study Torah. (3) Simlai said: the important mitzvah is to seek God, to live by one's faith. All three were seeking to answer the same question.

There are, then, three basic commandments: love of neighbor, study of Torah, love of God. We have little trouble with the mitzvah to deal fairly with our neighbors, with other people. We can make sense of what it means to study Torah. But what about loving God? Can you really be commanded to love? Isn't love something that must be given freely, because you want to give it?

To find the answer to that question, to explore the mitzvot that deal with us and God, we will turn to the prayers we say. For it is through prayer that we speak to God. In prayer we speak of our attitudes and feelings for God. Prayer is an important part of the celebration of bar and bat mitzvah, so it is only fitting that we turn now to what prayer can teach us about mitzvah.

GOD LOVES US, SO GOD TEACHES US

The Torah is about God's love for Israel, the Jewish people. It is a long love letter. The word "love" must appear more times, in more ways, than any other word in our *Siddur*, the Prayer Book. So we have to ask about how God loves us through giving the mitzvot. To do so, we turn to the prayer that says it all, all in one place. It is called *Ahavah Rabbah*: "Deep is Your love for us."

Ahavah Rabbah—the name of the prayer comes from its first two words—mixes together several ideas: God's love, God's teaching us the laws of life, our trust in God. We ask for something in this prayer; indeed, we beg for it. We plead that we be allowed to learn God's laws and that we enjoy understanding. We ask God to give us the will to study Torah and to carry out its teachings.

At the end comes a message not only for the individual Jew but also for all Israel. We ask God to bring us back to the Holy Land. God has chosen us and loves us and, therefore, we ask God to do this for us. That is the final part of the picture: God chooses Israel and loves Israel, the Jewish people.

And how do we know? The answer is already in our hands: because God gives the Torah, because God gives the mitzvot for us to do. God, who loves us, wants much from us. God, who loves us, gives much to us.

Ahavah Rabbah

Deep is Your love for us, O Lord our God; Your compassion and tenderness is great. Our Parent our Ruler, our ancestors trusted in You and You taught them the laws of life. For their sake, be gracious to us and teach us.

Parent, Creator of mercy, have mercy upon us. Guide us to know and to understand; to heed, learn, and teach; to obey, perform, and uphold all the teachings of Your Torah with love.

Make our eyes bright with Your Torah, make our hearts cling to Your mitzvot. Unite our hearts in the love and awe of Your name.

Then we shall never be brought to shame. For in Your holy name, great and awesome One, we shall trust. We shall rejoice and delight in Your help.

Now bring us safely from the four corners of the earth, and lead us proudly to our holy land.

For You are the Maker of deliverance; You have chosen us from among all peoples and tongues; You have drawn us near to Your greatness—for which we praise and thank You in truth—in order that we might thank You and proclaim Your Oneness with love.

Blessed are You, O Lord, who has chosen the people Israel through love.

The point of this prayer, clearly, is that God loves us; therefore, God gives us Torah and commandments. We pray, when we say this prayer, that God will love us by giving us the power to learn the Torah and do the commandments. So the mitzvot are a sign of God's love for us, for Israel.

The celebration of your becoming a bat or bar mitzvah is a time of love. People come from far and wide to join in celebrating—relatives, friends, your parent or parents, teachers, brothers, sisters. It is your day. It is a way people have of showing their love for you. Of course, what truly makes it your day is a change in you and in your position in the family and in the synagogue and in the community of Israel.

More About Love

Your parents love you; that is why they care what you do. Since they care, they give you lots of orders: Do this, don't do that. They pile up many things they want you to do or not to do. Parents are mitzvah-factories.

Teachers also care for you; they pay attention to what you say or do. When you are right, they praise you. When you are wrong, they tell you. They, too, give many mitzvot.

The Teaching

From the Prayer Book

אַהֲבָה רַבָּה אֲהַבְתָּנוּ יְיָ
אֱלֹהֵינוּ, חֶמְלָה גְדוֹלָה
וִיתֵרָה חָמַלְתָּ עָלֵינוּ. אָבִינוּ
מַלְכֵּנוּ, בַּעֲבוּר אֲבוֹתֵינוּ
שֶׁבָּטְחוּ בְךָ, וַתְּלַמְּדֵם חֻקֵּי
חַיִּים, כֵּן תְּחָנֵּנוּ וּתְלַמְּדֵנוּ.
אָבִינוּ הָאָב הָרַחֲמָן,
הַמְרַחֵם, רַחֵם עָלֵינוּ, וְתֵן
בְּלִבֵּנוּ לְהָבִין וּלְהַשְׂכִּיל,
לִשְׁמֹעַ לִלְמֹד וּלְלַמֵּד,
לִשְׁמֹר וְלַעֲשׂוֹת, וּלְקַיֵּם
אֶת־כָּל־דִּבְרֵי תַלְמוּד
תוֹרָתֶךָ, בְּאַהֲבָה.
וְהָאֵר עֵינֵינוּ בְּתוֹרָתֶךָ,
וְדַבֵּק לִבֵּנוּ בְּמִצְוֹתֶיךָ, וְיַחֵד
לְבָבֵנוּ לְאַהֲבָה וּלְיִרְאָה שְׁמֶךָ,
וְלֹא נֵבוֹשׁ לְעוֹלָם וָעֶד.
כִּי בְשֵׁם קָדְשְׁךָ הַגָּדוֹל
וְהַנּוֹרָא בָּטָחְנוּ, נָגִילָה
וְנִשְׂמְחָה, בִּישׁוּעָתֶךָ.
וַהֲבִיאֵנוּ לְשָׁלוֹם מֵאַרְבַּע
כַּנְפוֹת הָאָרֶץ, וְתוֹלִיכֵנוּ
קוֹמְמִיּוּת לְאַרְצֵנוּ, כִּי אֵל
פּוֹעֵל יְשׁוּעוֹת אָתָּה, וּבָנוּ
בָחַרְתָּ מִכָּל־עַם וְלָשׁוֹן,
וְקֵרַבְתָּנוּ לְשִׁמְךָ הַגָּדוֹל
סֶלָה, בֶּאֱמֶת, לְהוֹדוֹת לְךָ
וּלְיַחֶדְךָ בְּאַהֲבָה.
בָּרוּךְ אַתָּה יְיָ, הַבּוֹחֵר
בְּעַמּוֹ יִשְׂרָאֵל בְּאַהֲבָה.

Deep is Your love for us, O Lord our God; Your compassion and tenderness is great. Our Parent our Ruler, our ancestors trusted in You and You taught them the laws of life. For their sake, be gracious to us and teach us.

Parent, Creator of mercy, have mercy upon us. Guide us to know and to understand; to heed, learn, and teach; to obey, perform, and uphold all the teachings of Your Torah with love.

Make our eyes bright with Your Torah, make our hearts cling to Your mitzvot. Unite our hearts in the love and awe of Your name.

Then we shall never be brought to shame. For in Your holy name, great and awesome One, we shall trust. We shall rejoice and delight in Your help.

Now bring us safely from the four corners of the earth, and lead us proudly to our holy land.

For You are the Maker of deliverance; You have chosen us from among all peoples and tongues; You have drawn us near to Your greatness—for which we praise and thank You in truth—in order that we might thank You and proclaim Your Oneness with love.

Blessed are You, O Lord, who has chosen the people Israel through love.

God is the parent and the teacher of Israel, our people. God is the parent, loving Israel. God is the teacher, instructing Israel. God gives Israel a great many instructions—mitzvot—in the Torah and along with the Torah. All this because God loves Israel.

By seeing the ways in which God is like your parent or teacher, you may begin to get some sense of the full idea of mitzvot. God's love for Israel leads God to command Israel. And each Israelite, each Jew, is subject to these mitzvot. But what good is being commanded, if we do not know what the commands mean? We must be taught, too. Through instruction comes knowledge of what we are supposed to do.

When we know what we are supposed to do and when we know that the commands come out of love, then we receive mitzvot. Being responsible to keep these mitzvot, as you know already, means being a bar or bat mitzvah.

Why God Gives Mitzvot

We discuss commandments by talking of Torah. We talk of Torah and find ourselves speaking about God who gives the Torah. These things go together: God, Torah, mitzvah. Along with them go other words like "laws of life," and "understanding." There are many words which are very close in meaning, and which we use to serve the same purpose.

Yet when we collect these words and make a list of them—God, Torah, mitzvah, learning, laws of life, understanding, upholding—a large question remains. Why does God give mitzvot? What is the purpose of learning Torah? Are the laws of life good, neutral, or bad? What makes everything work together? In what way are all these words keys to the same gate?

In the prayer that we read before the *Shema*, the prayer called Ahavah Rabbah, one word is used time and again. It is the word love. Many other words in the prayer are place markers for the word love. When God has mercy on us, it is by giving us the power "to know and to understand." We ask God to "make our eyes bright" with Torah; to "unite our hearts." These are words that lovers use.

Now we must ask, what evidence do we have from within our faith that God loves us? The answer, this prayer tells us, is Torah and mitzvot. The answer bring us right back where we started. Because God loves us, therefore God pays attention to what we think, say, and do. Because God loves us, therefore God cares what we think, say, and do. Without the love, the concern would not be there.

Full circle

Just as the prayer has come full circle—starting with the idea that God loves us, telling of how God shows love by giving us commandments, and ending with the fact that God's commandments are a proof of God's love—so, too, we have come full circle in a way.

We began by speaking of the changes taking place in you and of how you have reached a new place of responsibility in Israel, the Jewish people. This is happening because you are becoming a special you, a person that no one else can ever become. Even though you will always be a part of your family, you are drawing apart from it, too.

Now, just as you are becoming the only one in control of you, you are told that bar or bat mitzvah means becoming commanded. What a striking problem: the last thing you want is more orders. On the other hand, truly to become yourself, you must be responsible for yourself. You have a whole new set of orders to carry out, that is, commandments to fulfill. And the sign of that, the sign of your new place as a full member of the Jewish people, is your bat or bar mitzvah.

God's love for you, your parents' devotion to you, your teachers' caring for you—these are one light through three prisms. They are the waters of one ocean, washing up on three beaches. When we speak of God, we have only our words as human beings, our experiences in this world. But these words, these experiences, are what we are, and they are all that we are. We offer to the One who made us what that One has made. We have no more than ourselves to give. But more than that is not needed. The love that formed us, the love that nurtures us and teaches us and tells us what to do and what not to do in this world, in our lives—that is the closest we can come to understanding God's love.

To become a bat mitzvah or a bar mitzvah without speaking about love would be like celebrating your birthday but forgetting your name.

LOOKING BACK, LOOKING FORWARD

These are the main points in this chapter: (1) God's love for Israel is deep. We know that because God taught Israel the laws of life. (2) Israel asks God for the will to study Torah, to listen to its words, to carry out the mitzvot. (3) Parents love us, so they care about what we do. That is why a parent gives orders about what to do and what not to do. (4) Teachers care for us. They show their care by paying attention to what we say and do, by praising us when we are right and correcting our mistakes when we are wrong. (5) A mitzvah is a sign that God cares for us. It shows that God cares what we say, what we do, what we think, and how we feel. (6) Love is one thing, though it may take many forms. God's love, a parent's love, a grandparent's love, a teacher's concern, a coach's caring—all these are different, yet the same.

The logical next question is how can we take so much without giving something in return? Is something not asked of us? We speak of God's deep love for us; and we compare the love of a parent or grandparent or aunt or coach or friend to the love of God for us. So we stand at the center and everyone brings us the gifts of love. But in real life you love others as they love you. So we must ask, What about loving God? Where does the love we feel for God fit into the commandments? The answer, as the next chapter tells, is that loving God is the first and foremost of the commandments.

THE MAIN MITZVAH: TO LOVE GOD

When we try to understand what God wants of us—Torah, mitzvot—we turn to our own world as a mirror of God's world. We compare God's concern for us to the concern of teachers and parents. Commandments are a sign of caring, a sign of love. And they are a way of sharing.

If you know something worthwhile, you want to share it with someone else. The pleasure of knowing is in telling, as much as in understanding. Torah stands for what God knows and wants us to know: "revelation," that is, teaching from God for us. The prayer we studied in the last chapter, Ahavah Rabbah, "Deep Love," is a song about how if God loves us, God will give us the ability to

understand Torah and mitzvot. So, Torah and mitzvot—
revelation and commandments—are both signs of God's
loving and caring.

Now, using what we learn in this world as a mirror
for God's world, we have no difficulty in understanding
the Shema. For the Shema contains the great commandment of Judaism, to love God with all our heart, with all
our soul, with all our might. And to teach that love to
other people and to talk about that love everywhere and
all the time; to write those words of love and put them as a
sign upon our hands and to tie them as a mark between
our eyes, as we do ritually with *tefillin*; and to copy those
words and put them on the doorposts of our houses, as we
do ritually with *mezuzot*.

What an extraordinary demand! Yet how natural.
For God lavishes love on us. God then demands love from
us. It is as simple as that. From this one command, to
love, come all these: Torah, to be taught and talked
about; tefillin, a garment of love; mezuzot, markers of
love that say here is a place where God is loved.

Shema

Hear, O Israel: The Lord is our God, the Lord is One.

*Blessed be His Name, whose glorious kingdom is forever
and ever.*

*You shall love the Lord your God with all your heart,
with all your soul, and with all your might. Let these
words which I command you this day be in your heart.
You shall teach them diligently to your children; and*

you shall speak of them when you are sitting in your home and when you are walking along the road, as you are lying down to rest and as you are awakening.

You shall bind them as a sign upon your hand; let them be as frontlets between your eyes. And you shall write them on the doorposts of your homes and upon your gates.

A moment ago I said that the Shema is perfectly natural. For if God loves us, then we must love God. Yet there is something puzzling here, too. For the Shema is not a statement of facts: God loves you, so you must love God. The Shema is a commandment: *You shall love God.*

Being Commanded to Love

A command is not the same thing as a statement of how things are. A command goes beyond the facts to say how things shall be. A command addressed to you tells what you must do. In this form, there is nothing to negotiate. When you command, you expect to be obeyed. You want not merely response. You want obedience. That is why you command instead of asking, requesting, pleading, arguing, or stating.

A command is special. And what is commanded here is also special, and it is something that cannot be commanded: love.

For love is not something to be had merely for the asking. The other person has to feel it, has to bring it up out of the depths of being. You can command others to do something outwardly. But can you command love?

The Teaching

From the Prayer Book (Deuteronomy 6:4–9)

שְׁמַע יִשְׂרָאֵל יְהוָֹה אֱלֹהֵינוּ
יְהוָֹה אֶחָד.

בָּרוּךְ שֵׁם כְּבוֹד מַלְכוּתוֹ
לְעוֹלָם וָעֶד.

וְאָהַבְתָּ אֵת יְהוָֹה אֱלֹהֶיךָ
בְּכָל־לְבָבְךָ וּבְכָל־נַפְשְׁךָ
וּבְכָל־מְאֹדֶךָ. וְהָיוּ הַדְּבָרִים
הָאֵלֶּה אֲשֶׁר אָנֹכִי מְצַוְּךָ
הַיּוֹם עַל־לְבָבֶךָ. וְשִׁנַּנְתָּם
לְבָנֶיךָ וְדִבַּרְתָּ בָּם בְּשִׁבְתְּךָ
בְּבֵיתֶךָ וּבְלֶכְתְּךָ בַדֶּרֶךְ
וּבְשָׁכְבְּךָ וּבְקוּמֶךָ.

וּקְשַׁרְתָּם לְאוֹת עַל־יָדֶךָ
וְהָיוּ לְטֹטָפֹת בֵּין עֵינֶיךָ.
וּכְתַבְתָּם עַל־מְזֻזוֹת בֵּיתֶךָ
וּבִשְׁעָרֶיךָ.

Hear, O Israel: The Lord is our God, the Lord is One.

Blessed be His name, whose glorious kingdom is forever and ever.

You shall love the Lord your God with all your heart, with all you soul, and with all your might. Let these words which I command you this day be in your heart. You shall teach them diligently to your children; and you shall speak of them when you are sitting in your home and when you are walking along the road, as you are lying down to rest and as you are awakening.

You shall bind them as a sign upon your hand; let them be as frontlets between your eyes. And you shall write them on the doorposts of your homes and upon your gates.

Obedience to the mitzvot means doing the mitzvot in the way they are meant to be done. It means carrying out one action and not some other. It means not doing some things and doing some others. If all the mitzvot required were actions, then the life of Torah would be a life of easy agreement with what is asked of us. Indeed, in a way, it would be a life of enslavement.

So the first mitzvah—the command to love—concerns not what we do, but why we do it. It speaks of how we feel, our attitudes about ourselves and what we do. It asks us to look inside ourselves and discover the answers to some very basic questions: Are our feelings and attitudes things we control? Or are these not just responses to the world around us?

Can You Shape Your Feelings?

We do have some control about how we feel. We do not feel merely what the world tells us to feel. Emotions are not simply things that happen to you. Some of the time, in some ways, they are things that you can make happen. For example, you can put yourself in a good mood by thinking of things you like. Likewise, you can put yourself into a bad mood by thinking of unhappy things. If you take everything to heart and treat everything that is said to you as important, you may end up feeling upset much of the time. If you have confidence in yourself and know that you are good and important, no matter what others say to you, then you will end up feeling proud of yourself and happy much of the time.

A lot depends upon what you do. Because we are what we do. What we do shapes how we feel as much as how we feel shapes what we do. If you do things you think you should not do, you may feel good for a moment, then bad for a long time. If you take a chance with drugs or liquor, or if you do with another boy or girl things you think you should not, then you will feel guilty, you will feel badly about yourself. In this way, we are what we do.

This brings us back to the commandment to love, to feel something. Now you can see that it is possible to be commanded to feel happy, or to feel sad, or to feel proud, or to feel guilty. The reason is that you can be commanded to do certain things, and in turn these things help you to feel in certain ways. Our actions influence our feelings.

You Control Your Feelings

The commandment to love says that you can control how you feel. If you can be told to love, then you are held—by the One God who tells you—to be in command of yourself. It is a statement of respect for you. For the statement of the Shema—the command to love—says much about human beings and what we are.

The Shema says we can be commanded to respond to love with love because our feelings and attitudes are our own, just as much as our deeds. You agree that if you do something wrong you are responsible. You know, too, that there are feelings you would not want to share with others, feelings or attitudes that are wrong. All of us have these feelings—hidden desires, unacceptable dreams. They are a part of our very being.

For example, at times you feel jealousy of a brother or a sister. You want everything for yourself. But you have to share. You might feel envy of a friend in school who is smarter than you, or a better athlete, or a finer musician. These are not feelings you express with pride. True, you may express them. But in secret ways.

The commandment to love says that you can control your feelings and attitudes. True, you cannot totally master them. No one can. It would not be good for you if you tried. Even if you pretend not to feel things you really do feel, the feelings would still be there. The hatred, the envy, the jealousy, the fear, the sense of not being able to do what you want or be what you want—all would still be there. But you can do things with these feelings and attitudes just as you can do things with your ability and power to act. You need not be controlled by feelings—you are not a prisoner of your heart or a victim of the impulse of the moment.

When the Shema says, "You shall love," the Shema claims you have the power to take your heart and your soul and your might and do what you will with them. You know you can make decisions about many things—what food you will eat, how you will dress, what you will do on one day as against some other. It is a mitzvah to eat *matzah* on Passover. You know you can decide to do that, to obey that commandment. The Shema says it is a mitzvah to love God. What the Shema says is quite a compliment to you.

Strong Feelings

One way that controlling your emotions is important

is in your feelings about sexuality. Coming to a time of sexual maturity is a moment of strong emotions. You now have powers you did not know existed. You feel things you did not know were there to be felt. Your body sends you messages you are not sure you wish to hear just yet. And all of this is happening to you whether or not you want it to.

Becoming a bar or bat mitzvah is a part of this same critical turning in your life. Here, too, are strong feelings, feelings of pride in your own accomplishment and of thankfulness to your parents, brothers and sisters, rabbi and teachers. How can you deal with all of these important events and strong feelings in yourself as a person and in your place in the community?

The first thing to know is that you *can* deal with how you feel. You do not have to say, "I can't help it, it's just how I feel." You can say, "I *can* help it. It's how I feel, but I have the power to change how I feel, just as I have the power to change my mind."

Through doing certain things, you can teach yourself to feel certain things. For what you do expresses how you feel. So what you do can give you habits that in the end will affect how you feel. The point of the mitzvot is not merely to make us follow slavishly one pattern of living rather than some other. The point is to set us free inside, to teach us how to change and control ourselves. The purpose of the mitzvot is to educate our hearts. The mitzvot serve to purify our hearts to love God. That is the simple message of the Shema.

As soon as the Shema says to love God it hastens to add: put on clothing of love of God, live in a house marked by love of God, talk wherever you are about love of God. So the Shema contains the message. If you feel a certain way, you must do certain things. If you do these things, then you have a chance of feeling a certain way. The mitzvot are our school of life. They have the power to shape not just what we do, but how we feel about what we do, how we feel about ourselves—and, therefore, how we feel about God.

In truth, no one can command your love. It is yours to give. That is why God commands us to love God, as God loves us. In the end, there is only the respect, the hopefulness, represented by the mitzvah to love God with all our heart, with all our soul, with all our might. These things—heart, soul, might—are ours to offer up. God can command. But we are free to obey or not to obey, to give or to hold back. How we respond to God's command will determine who and what we are, who and what we want to be.

LOOKING BACK, LOOKING FORWARD

These are the main points of this chapter: (1) Through doing certain things you can teach yourself to feel in certain ways. (2) The mitzvot tell us to do certain things. They teach our hearts the things that can be done to make us feel certain ways. (3) The main attitude the mitzvot teach us to have in our hearts—the feeling taught by the Shema—is love of God. (4) The fact that God wants us to love God means that God cares for us. We are all important to God. So God commands us with the Shema, "You shall love the Lord your God with all your heart, with all your soul, and with all your might." (5) Love is not something you can demand or command. But by giving us the mitzvot God tells us to do the things that will lead us to love God. (6) The mitzvot are marks of God's respect for us. Each one is a reminder that God knows we have the ability to shape and control ourselves. (7) Becoming a bat mitzvah or a bar mitzvah means that we can deal with how we feel as much as with what we do.

The Shema presents the great commandment to love God. In Conservative and Orthodox prayer books, the Shema continues in two further paragraphs. One tells of the rewards and punishments attached to the commandments. The other speaks of *tsitsit*, show-fringes, worn on the *tallit* or prayer shawl. If you are a Reform Jew, you will find the next chapter informative but not necessarily relevant to your own life as a Jew. If you are Orthodox, Reconstructionist, or Conservative, the prayers about the mitzvot in the next chapter are central to your life as a Jew. In either case, what they teach us about mitzvot is important to all Jews.

THE YOKE OF THE MITZVOT

As we know, the Shema gives us a complete statement on the mitzvot, starting with the mitzvah to love God, ending with the reference to all the mitzvot together. This statement on the mitzvot is called the "yoke of the mitzvot," and when we recite it, we are said to accept upon ourselves the "yoke of the mitzvot." Here are the last two parts of the statement:

(1) It will come to pass, if you will listen carefully to My commandments that I have given to you this day, to love the Lord your God and to serve Him with all your heart and with all your soul; then I will give rain to your land in the proper season—autumn rain and spring rain— and you will harvest your grain, your wine, and your

oil. I will provide grass in your fields for your cattle. So you will eat and be contented.

Take care lest you be tempted [to forsake God], to turn to false gods and worship them. For then God's anger will be turned against you. God will close up the heavens and there will be no rain; the earth will not give up its produce. And you will soon disappear from the good land which the Lord gives you.

Therefore, place these words of Mine within your heart and within your soul. Bind them as a sign upon your hand; let them be frontlets between your eyes. Teach them to your children, speaking of them in your home and when you are walking along the road, as you are lying down to rest and as you are awakening. Write them on the doorposts of your homes and upon your gates. Then your days and the days of your children will be as great in number upon the land which the Lord promised to your ancestors as the days of all the heavens upon the earth.

(2) The Lord spoke to Moses, saying, Tell the people of Israel they shall make tsitsit [show-fringes] on the corners of their clothing for all generations to come, and they shall place on each of the corner fringes a thread of blue.

And these shall be your fringes: when you see them you will be reminded of all the Lord's commandments and you will do them. Then you will not be led astray by your desires or the things your eyes wish to seize improperly.

So you will remember and do all My commandments. You will be holy before your God.

I am the Lord your God who brought you out of the land of Egypt to be your God. I, the Lord, am your God.

The "Yoke of the Commandments"

These words—and the saying of them—place upon us the "yoke of the commandments." This word, "yoke," is meant to call something to our minds. It is an analogy or metaphor, that is, it compares one thing with another.

A yoke guides an ox in its ploughing. Being in a "yoke" means being guided or directed. That is, a yoke serves as a metaphor for discipline. When you take upon yourself the "yoke of the mitzvot" you do so freely. But once you do so, you are subject to the disciplines of the mitzvot. Now you know that the first of these disciplines, these training-rules, concerns your feelings. This is because your feelings are the hardest thing to bring under control, to shape in the way you want them shaped. But there are other parts of life that are equally subject to guidance or discipline.

This matter of discipline may be troubling you. When I become a bar mitzvah or bat mitzvah, am I no longer free to do whatever I want? Do I give up more than I get?

No, you are no longer free to do whatever you want—if you ever were. You increase in independence, but also in responsibility. You now make your own choices, but more is at stake in each choice. When you were younger you had many preferences, but in fact you

made few choices of your own. Now that your are teen-
aged, you also are challenged to become something you
could not be before.

Freedom to Choose

There is this new freedom before you. But freedom is to
be used. Being free to choose does not leave you free to
avoid choosing. Whatever you do or do not do, things will
happen. So the freedom you now enter is a freedom to
make certain choices. Once these choices are made, you
become responsible for them, and for what happens
because of them. If you choose to be lazy, you will give up
other choices you may have wanted to make. You will
never have the patience to carry through things you really
want to do. You will have high hopes that seldom will be
met. You will shape large dreams with little chance of
having them come true.

Even now you know that if you want to do something, whether it is in sports or music or school, it takes
work. If you want to learn a subject at school it takes
drill, concentration, repetition. If you want to become a
good athlete, it takes practice. If you want to become a
good musician, you have to work at it. You are free to
choose. But once you choose—to do, not to do—many
things follow surely. The real choice before you now is to
make choices. You are not free to avoid making choices
any longer.

The picture of us as people who accept the "yoke
of the commandments" shows that we can freely choose

to accept the mitzvot each day, each time we say the Shema. Every *Shabbat* we must choose whether or not to make the day holy. Yet each choice makes the next one easier or harder. And, within the disciplines of the commandments, as we shall see later on, doing one mitzvah makes the next one more natural. The discipline reshapes us—we remake ourselves from day to day.

The Shema and the Commandments

The two paragraphs we are studying in this chapter are made up of two passages from the Torah: Deuteronomy 11:13–21 and Numbers 15:37–41. Both refer to the mitzvot in general. The first makes the point that if you do the commandments you will be rewarded, and if you do not keep the commandments you will suffer. The second speaks of tsitsit and then makes the point that when you keep the mitzvot you will not be led to do whatever you desire just because you desire it.

This section of the Shema paints a picture of the world as we might *want* it to be. But we are going to have to think carefully to make sense of what this says in the world as we *know* it to be. For the Shema says that if you keep the mitzvot then the important things in life will go well. In the language of the Bible, there will be rain in autumn and in spring, when the Land of Israel needs the rain. If you do not keep the mitzvot, there will be no rain and the earth will not yield a crop. In other words, there is a simple reward for doing what is asked, and a simple punishment for not doing it.

The Teaching

וְהָיָה אִם־שָׁמֹעַ תִּשְׁמְעוּ
אֶל־מִצְוֹתַי אֲשֶׁר אָנֹכִי
מְצַוֶּה אֶתְכֶם הַיּוֹם לְאַהֲבָה
אֶת־יְהֹוָה אֱלֹהֵיכֶם וּלְעָבְדוֹ
בְּכָל־לְבַבְכֶם וּבְכָל־
נַפְשְׁכֶם. וְנָתַתִּי מְטַר־
אַרְצְכֶם בְּעִתּוֹ יוֹרֶה
וּמַלְקוֹשׁ וְאָסַפְתָּ דְגָנֶךָ
וְתִירֹשְׁךָ וְיִצְהָרֶךָ. וְנָתַתִּי
עֵשֶׂב בְּשָׂדְךָ לִבְהֶמְתֶּךָ
וְאָכַלְתָּ וְשָׂבָעְתָּ.
הִשָּׁמְרוּ לָכֶם פֶּן־יִפְתֶּה
לְבַבְכֶם וְסַרְתֶּם וַעֲבַדְתֶּם
אֱלֹהִים אֲחֵרִים
וְהִשְׁתַּחֲוִיתֶם לָהֶם. וְחָרָה
אַף־יְהֹוָה בָּכֶם וְעָצַר אֶת־
הַשָּׁמַיִם וְלֹא־יִהְיֶה מָטָר
וְהָאֲדָמָה לֹא תִתֵּן אֶת־
יְבוּלָהּ וַאֲבַדְתֶּם מְהֵרָה
מֵעַל הָאָרֶץ הַטֹּבָה אֲשֶׁר
יְהֹוָה נֹתֵן לָכֶם.
וְשַׂמְתֶּם אֶת־דְּבָרַי אֵלֶּה
עַל־לְבַבְכֶם וְעַל־נַפְשְׁכֶם
וּקְשַׁרְתֶּם אֹתָם לְאוֹת עַל־
יֶדְכֶם וְהָיוּ לְטוֹטָפֹת בֵּין
עֵינֵיכֶם. וְלִמַּדְתֶּם אֹתָם
אֶת־בְּנֵיכֶם לְדַבֵּר בָּם
בְּשִׁבְתְּךָ בְּבֵיתֶךָ וּבְלֶכְתְּךָ
בַדֶּרֶךְ וּבְשָׁכְבְּךָ וּבְקוּמֶךָ.

It will come to pass, if you will listen carefully to My commandments that I have given to you this day, to love the Lord your God and to serve Him with all your heart and with all your soul; then I will give rain to your land in the proper season—autumn rain and spring rain—and you will harvest your grain, your wine, and your oil. I will provide grass in your fields for your cattle. So you will eat and be contented.

Take care lest you be tempted [to forsake God], to turn to false gods and worship them. For then God's anger will be turned against you. God will close up the heavens and there will be no rain; the earth will not give up its produce. And you will soon disappear from the good land which the Lord gives you.

Therefore, place these words of Mine within your heart and within your soul. Bind them as a sign upon your hand; let them be frontlets between your eyes. Teach them to your children, speaking of them in your home and when you are walking along the road, as you are lying down

From the Prayer Book (Deuteronomy 11:13–21, Numbers 15:37–41)

וּכְתַבְתָּם עַל־מְזוּזוֹת בֵּיתֶךָ
וּבִשְׁעָרֶיךָ. לְמַעַן יִרְבּוּ
יְמֵיכֶם וִימֵי בְנֵיכֶם עַל
הָאֲדָמָה אֲשֶׁר נִשְׁבַּע יְהֹוָה
לַאֲבֹתֵיכֶם לָתֵת לָהֶם כִּימֵי
הַשָּׁמַיִם עַל־הָאָרֶץ.

וַיֹּאמֶר יְהֹוָה אֶל־מֹשֶׁה
לֵּאמֹר. דַּבֵּר אֶל־בְּנֵי
יִשְׂרָאֵל וְאָמַרְתָּ אֲלֵהֶם
וְעָשׂוּ לָהֶם צִיצִת עַל־כַּנְפֵי
בִגְדֵיהֶם לְדֹרֹתָם וְנָתְנוּ עַל־
צִיצִת הַכָּנָף פְּתִיל תְּכֵלֶת.
וְהָיָה לָכֶם לְצִיצִת
וּרְאִיתֶם אֹתוֹ וּזְכַרְתֶּם אֶת־
כָּל־מִצְוֹת יְהֹוָה וַעֲשִׂיתֶם
אֹתָם וְלֹא־תָתוּרוּ אַחֲרֵי
לְבַבְכֶם וְאַחֲרֵי עֵינֵיכֶם
אֲשֶׁר־אַתֶּם זֹנִים אַחֲרֵיהֶם.
לְמַעַן תִּזְכְּרוּ וַעֲשִׂיתֶם
אֶת־כָּל־מִצְוֹתָי וִהְיִיתֶם
קְדֹשִׁים לֵאלֹהֵיכֶם.
אֲנִי יְהֹוָה אֱלֹהֵיכֶם אֲשֶׁר
הוֹצֵאתִי אֶתְכֶם מֵאֶרֶץ
מִצְרַיִם לִהְיוֹת לָכֶם
לֵאלֹהִים אֲנִי יְהֹוָה
אֱלֹהֵיכֶם.

to rest and as you are awakening. Write them on the doorposts of your homes and upon your gates. Then your days and the days of your children will be as great in number upon the land which the Lord promised to your ancestors as the days of all the heavens upon the earth.

The Lord spoke to Moses, saying, Tell the people of Israel they shall make tsitsit on the corners of their clothing for all generations to come, and they shall place on each of the corner fringes a thread of blue.

And these shall be your fringes: when you see them you will be reminded of all the Lord's commandments and you will do them. Then you will not be led astray by your desires or the things your eyes wish to seize improperly.

So you will remember and do all My commandments. You will be holy before your God.

I am the Lord your God who brought you out of the land of Egypt to be your God. I, the Lord, am your God.

The World As We Wish It

You do not have to live many years to realize that this is not really how things happen. We wish that it were! But there is no automatic reward for doing good; and there is no automatic punishment for doing evil. You probably know people who cheat in school and get away with it. They may even feel good about it. You know that holy and pious people die, just as do ordinary and mean people. You know there is suffering in the world—and not just in the world in general, but in hospitals and old people's homes and even among young people. You know, too, that suffering is passed out in portions not cut to the size of a person's goodness or evil.

You know that the Jewish people in this world is not everywhere honored, respected, appreciated. Right now about a third of the American people hold bad opinions about the Jews—whatever the kind of Jews they know, or even if they know no Jews at all. And prejudice directed toward us does not see any difference between Jews who keep the mitzvot, or try to, and Jews who do not.

So the Shema here raises more questions than it answers. That is why it is omitted from the prayer books of the Reform and Reconstructionist synagogues and temples. It makes claims that some Jews simply cannot accept.

The World As It Is

Yet even if you do not recite these paragraphs, you cannot run away from the questions. Even if you do not say that the main commandment of love comes along with its own reward and punishment, there remains a problem. Does loving God do any good, if the lover still suffers and dies, as we know happens, no matter what? What good is all this love, this Deep Love, and what value is this Torah, and what benefit are these commandments?

Coming to the age of the mitzvot as you are, you might as well accept the simple fact that there is no straightforward answer to the question posed by pain, suffering, and death. There is no easy way to make sense of the position of Israel, the Jewish people, in this world. There is no way to come to grips with the events of our own century, the suffering and death of some six million Jews in Europe under the Nazis in World War II. There is no simple answer to why the Jewish state, the State of Israel, has to fight for survival in an unfriendly world. The promise of the Shema is not yet kept so far as the Shema says that those who keep the mitzvot will enjoy not only God's love but also worldly signs of God's love.

Perhaps this sad truth is one of our own making. We are the ones who think that if there is love there must be marks of love that we can understand and grasp. That is a perfectly natural expectation. But God is beyond, not in, nature. We are the ones who give and expect to get, who see the mitzvot as a means of exchange, a coin for purchasing better times.

It may be that in some long-term view, that is what the mitzvot are. But the promise of the mitzvot is not going to be kept for you if you think of it as a fair exchange. Your doing mitzvot does not make God do what you want—the mitzvot stand for your doing what God wants. The mitzvot are not good for you. You do not keep them because you feel like it. You keep mitzvot because God has commanded you.

The Sin of Giving Up, the Mitzvah of Hope

It is our lot in life to do these things, to be what we are. The only reward we have is the knowledge, from the Torah, that against it all, despite it all, God loves us and we are commanded to love God—and to act in the discipline of that love. Remember how Yohanan ben Zakkai phrases matters. He speaks of what we are created to do and to be. He does not speak of what we benefit from doing or being. He does not speak of reward. He speaks of living up to what we are made to become.

There never was a time in which the Shema's statements described everyday reality. When the Shema sees a connection between doing the commandments and enjoying an easy life, between not doing them and facing a hard life—it never looked out upon the real world of Israel, the Jewish people. The Shema was no easier to say before the destruction of the Jews of Europe in the Holocaust, or before someone you love died of cancer, than it is now. And it will never be easy. It has always raised a painful question for us as Jews, and it always will.

This is the true "yoke of the mitzvot." We have to accept the discipline of knowing that we seek to live a good and holy life without the certainty of reward "out there." It is what God wants of us and how God wants us to be. That is the only certainty. Everything else is hope.

But the hope is everything. The great commandment is to love God. The worst sin a Jew can commit is to despair, to give up. To love is to hope. To despair is to lose hope. You shall love the Lord your God—despite it all, against it all.

LOOKING BACK, LOOKING FORWARD

These are the main points of this chapter: (1) The second and third paragraphs of the Shema contain the promise that if you do the mitzvot the community will prosper; and if you do not do them it will suffer. (2) The "yoke of the commandments," expressed in these paragraphs, places a discipline upon us like the discipline of an athlete, a musician, an artist, or a writer. It is an effort that must be kept up day by day. (3) Reaching the age of mitzvot means that we have new freedoms, but also new disciplines—those of the mitzvot. It is the freedom, and the responsibility, to choose. (4) The choices you make have important consequences. The Shema outlines them in ways that present problems to us. The Shema says that if you do the commandments, you benefit. Yet we know that rewards cannot be expected in any immediate way. (5) The Shema and the paragraphs that go with it describe the world as it should be. The real choice is between love and despair.

Up to now we have spoken of the commandments in general. It is time to look at some specific mitzvot. The most important of these, after the commandment to love God, are presented in the *Aseret Hadibrot*, the "Ten Words," which we call the Ten Commandments.

THE TEN COMMANDMENTS

Until now we have spoken of mitzvot in general. You know that a mitzvah may concern something quite ordinary. What makes it a mitzvah is the power we have to feel or think in a special way as we do or avoid doing it. You also know that the prophets and rabbis of Israel, the Jewish people, tried to define the mitzvot by giving short lists of their main points—so they grouped the 613 mitzvot in 11 ways, in 3 ways, even in 1 single way. The Shema, with its stunning message that the main mitzvah is to love God, also talks in very general terms. It is time now to speak of actual mitzvot, to describe some examples of mitzvot one by one.

For that purpose there are many possible places to look both in the Bible and in the Talmud. But it is best to look at the most comprehensive, a list constructed at the head of many mitzvot. So we turn to the Ten Commandments, called in Hebrew *Aseret Hadibrot*, the "Ten Words."

The Ten Words

First, let us examine the Ten Commandments. Then we shall see how they apply to someone soon to become a bat or bar mitzvah, soon to become responsible for keeping them. Keep in mind that many people have spent their whole lives studying just these words, what they mean, how to apply them. So we want to remember just what we are looking for in them that is what they say to someone soon to have to obey them.

> *And God spoke all these words, saying:*
>
> *I am the Lord your God, who brought you out of the land of Egypt, out of the house of bondage.*
>
> *You shall have no other gods before Me. You shall not make for yourselves an idol, nor any kind of likeness, of any thing that is in heaven above, or that is on the earth beneath, or that is in the water below the earth. You shall not bow down to them, nor serve them. For I the Lord your God am a jealous God, visiting the evil ways of the parents upon the children even to the third and fourth generation of them that hate Me; and showing mercy even to the thousandth generation of them that love Me and keep My commandments.*

You shall not swear falsely by the name of the Lord your God. For the Lord will not hold that person guiltless that takes the Lord's name in vain.

Remember the sabbath day, to keep it holy. Six days shall you labor and do all your work, but the seventh day is a sabbath for the Lord your God. In it you shall not do any manner of work—you, nor your son, nor your daughter, nor your manservant, nor your maidservant, nor your cattle, nor the stranger that is within your gates—for in six days the Lord made heaven and earth, the sea, and all that is in them, and rested on the seventh day. For that reason, the Lord blessed the sabbath day, and made it holy.

Honor your father and your mother, so that your days may be long upon the land which the Lord you God gives you.

You shall not murder.
You shall not commit adultery.
You shall not steal.
You shall not testify falsely against your neighbor.
You shall not covet your neighbor's house; you shall not covet your neighbor's spouse, nor manservant, nor maidservant, nor ox, nor ass, nor any thing that is your neighbor's.

Charting the Commandments

It is useful to make a sort of chart of the Ten Commandments to see how they affect parts of our life. The first section of the chart looks like this:

I. Our relationship to God

    A. I am the Lord your God
    B. No other gods
        1. no statues of god
        2. no serving another god
    C. Do not take God's name in vain, meaning not to take false oaths using God's name as a proof

That last item is a bridge to what is coming next. Why? Because you take an oath—swear to another person— usually about something involving people. So we come to the second group of commandments:

II. Our relationship to the world

> **Remember the Sabbath day to keep it holy. Work for six days, rest on the seventh—you and your animals. God worked six days and rested on the seventh, so you make things for six days, then make the seventh day holy.**

This is one item, but it covers many things. It deals with how we conduct our lives, use our time, make things, and enjoy things. The commandment is in two main parts: (a) work; (b) rest. Without one, the other is incomplete. You work by making things. You rest by enjoying them. Both are vital. You work six days, changing things through study or through earning a living. You rest one day by not changing things, by enjoying the world. This great mitzvah comes to teach us something about our place in the order of nature. We pause, look around, look inward, and take time out to understand. In the prayer, Ahavah Rabbah, we ask to be taught "the laws of life." The word "life" here has a special meaning. It means "all life," nature, the world at large. The mitzvah of Sabbath observance is, all by itself, a great part of the answer to that prayer.

III. Our relationship to other people

A. Honor your father and mother
B. Do not murder
C. Do not commit adultery
D. Do not steal
E. Do not give false testimony or lie
F. Do not envy

These mitzvot are easy to accept; not always easy to do. It is easy to agree about honoring your father and your mother. But on an everyday basis, try it for twelve hours straight. That is, in the rough and tumble of dos and don'ts, try to remember that your parent or parents love you, even when they say No, or especially when they say No.

It is easy to agree not to murder. But the commandment teaches us more than that. It comes to remind us that every life is precious.

Sex

At this point in life, the command forbidding adultery is not relevant to you. It commands a married man and woman to remain completely loyal to one another, not to love anyone else as they love one another.

But your coming to sexual maturity is very much on your mind. So as you being to enter into manhood or womanhood, you must try to reckon with what the Torah has to say to you about this most important process in your growing up. What this commandment teaches is that there are mitzvot that deal with your role as a man or a woman, and with your relationship to the opposite sex.

These mitzvot may seem far-off since right now you may not be able to say to the world that the most important thing on your mind is the opposite sex. Yet you know that this is the opposite of the truth. One of the most important sides to your life as a human being will be your relationship to boys if you are a girl, or to girls if you are a boy. How you dress, the things you do with your free time, even the way you look at yourself in the mirror—all of these will be colored by your thinking of the opposite sex. Right now you may know plenty about the "plumbing" of sexuality, about the body's parts and how they operate. But you had best begin to think about the feelings, on the one side, and responsibilities, on the other.

Sex is one important result of love. So sex really does come into the great circle of feelings and emotions we faced when we studied the main commandment, to love God. You remember that we compared the feelings you have for your mother or father or both to your feelings for God; and we compared God's feelings for you—God's caring and concern and interest—with your father's or your mother's caring for you. These are expressions of love. You also know that because of sexual attraction, a very deep and powerful love comes into being between a man and a woman. Right now you see this in only the earlier phases, the buds that lead to the blossoms. Later in life you will see the fruit of love in marriage and in having and raising children. Until you are married, you are not a complete person. (That does not mean all marriages are good. Many do not work out. That is a sad fact. But all marriages begin in love and express love.)

For you, right now, the meaning of the commandment "not to commit adultery" is clear. So far as sex is subject to mitzvot, it must mean that your relationship to the opposite sex takes account of two things: (1) the respect you feel for yourself and the pride you take in yourself, and (2) the respect you owe to your girlfriend or boyfriend, as the case may be. Just as you do not wish to be used or abused by someone else, so you must not do such things to the other person. That, at least, is the beginning of the matter. There is much more to be learned about the mitzvot of love as they relate to the opposite sex. But not all mitzvot can be learned, or done, in one day.

Stealing

It is easy to agree not to steal, until you make a list of all the things you might steal. There's plenty of real, concrete stealing in the world, beginning with taking what doesn't belong to you, cheating on an examination, or even defacing a desk or a building that belongs to everybody. To steal is to claim as yours what is someone else's—or everyone else's. In a thousand small ways and large, from littering the public streets to robbing someone of a good

The Teaching

וַיְדַבֵּר אֱלֹהִים אֵת כָּל־
הַדְּבָרִים הָאֵלֶּה לֵאמֹר.
אָנֹכִי יְהוָה אֱלֹהֶיךָ אֲשֶׁר
הוֹצֵאתִיךָ מֵאֶרֶץ מִצְרַיִם
מִבֵּית עֲבָדִים.
לֹא־יִהְיֶה לְךָ אֱלֹהִים
אֲחֵרִים עַל־פָּנָי. לֹא־
תַעֲשֶׂה לְךָ פֶסֶל וְכָל־
תְּמוּנָה אֲשֶׁר בַּשָּׁמַיִם
מִמַּעַל וַאֲשֶׁר בָּאָרֶץ מִתַּחַת
וַאֲשֶׁר בַּמַּיִם מִתַּחַת לָאָרֶץ.
לֹא־תִשְׁתַּחֲוֶה לָהֶם וְלֹא
תָעָבְדֵם כִּי אָנֹכִי יְהוָה
אֱלֹהֶיךָ אֵל קַנָּא פֹּקֵד עֲוֹן
אָבֹת עַל־בָּנִים עַל־שִׁלֵּשִׁים
וְעַל־רִבֵּעִים לְשֹׂנְאָי. וְעֹשֶׂה
חֶסֶד לַאֲלָפִים לְאֹהֲבַי
וּלְשֹׁמְרֵי מִצְוֹתָי.
לֹא תִשָּׂא אֶת־שֵׁם־יְהוָה
אֱלֹהֶיךָ לַשָּׁוְא כִּי לֹא יְנַקֶּה
יְהוָה אֵת אֲשֶׁר־יִשָּׂא אֶת־
שְׁמוֹ לַשָּׁוְא.

And God spoke all these words, saying:

I am the Lord your God, who brought you out of the land of Egypt, out of the house of bondage.

You shall have no other gods before Me. You shall not make for yourselves an idol, nor any kind of likeness, of any thing that is in heaven above, or that is on the earth beneath, or that is in the water below the earth. You shall not bow down to them, nor serve them. For I the Lord your God am a jealous God, visiting the evil ways of the parents upon the children even to the third and fourth generation of them that hate Me; and showing mercy even to the thousandth generation of them that love Me and keep My commandments.

You shall not swear falsely by the name of the Lord your God. For the Lord will not hold that person guiltless that takes the Lord's name in vain.

From the Torah: Exodus 20:1–14

זָכוֹר אֶת־יוֹם הַשַּׁבָּת לְקַדְּשׁוֹ. שֵׁשֶׁת יָמִים תַּעֲבֹד וְעָשִׂיתָ כָּל־מְלַאכְתֶּךָ. וְיוֹם הַשְּׁבִיעִי שַׁבָּת לַיהוָה אֱלֹהֶיךָ לֹא תַעֲשֶׂה כָל־מְלָאכָה אַתָּה וּבִנְךָ־וּבִתֶּךָ עַבְדְּךָ וַאֲמָתְךָ וּבְהֶמְתֶּךָ וְגֵרְךָ אֲשֶׁר בִּשְׁעָרֶיךָ. כִּי שֵׁשֶׁת־יָמִים עָשָׂה יְהוָה אֶת־הַשָּׁמַיִם וְאֶת־הָאָרֶץ אֶת־הַיָּם וְאֶת־כָּל־אֲשֶׁר־בָּם וַיָּנַח בַּיּוֹם הַשְּׁבִיעִי עַל־כֵּן בֵּרַךְ יְהוָה אֶת־יוֹם הַשַּׁבָּת וַיְקַדְּשֵׁהוּ.

כַּבֵּד אֶת־אָבִיךָ וְאֶת־אִמֶּךָ לְמַעַן יַאֲרִכוּן יָמֶיךָ עַל הָאֲדָמָה אֲשֶׁר־יְהוָה אֱלֹהֶיךָ נֹתֵן לָךְ.

לֹא תִרְצָח

לֹא תִנְאָף

לֹא תִגְנֹב

לֹא־תַעֲנֶה בְרֵעֲךָ עֵד שָׁקֶר.

לֹא תַחְמֹד בֵּית רֵעֶךָ,
לֹא־תַחְמֹד אֵשֶׁת רֵעֶךָ
וְעַבְדּוֹ וַאֲמָתוֹ וְשׁוֹרוֹ
וַחֲמֹרוֹ וְכֹל אֲשֶׁר לְרֵעֶךָ.

Remember the sabbath day, to keep it holy. Six days shall you labor and do all your work, but the seventh days is a sabbath for the Lord your God. In it you shall not do any manner of work—you, nor your son, nor your daughter, nor your manservant, nor your maidservant, nor your cattle, nor the stranger that is within your gates—for in six days the Lord made heaven and earth, the sea, and all that is in them, and rested on the seventh day. For that reason, the Lord blessed the sabbath day, and made it holy.

Honor your father and your mother, so that your days may be long upon the land which the Lord your God gives you.

You shall not murder.
You shall not commit adultery.
You shall not steal.
You shall not testify falsely against your neighbor.

You shall not covet your neighbor's house; you shall not covet your neighbor's spouse, nor manservant, nor maidservant, nor ox, nor ass, nor any thing that is your neighbor's.

name by telling tales about them, it is more common than disrespect for a parent or even ignoring the Sabbath.

Lying

Then there is the commandment regarding lying. Yes, "bearing false witness" applies to everyday lying. Enough said.

Envy

The Ten Commandments end with envy—wanting badly what belongs to someone else. But envy, or coveting, can start an engine of bad feelings and bad actions that leads in the final stages to stealing or to murder. At your age there is probably no more urgent mitzvah than not envying someone else.

We all take our own measure by looking at other people. It is hard to accept yourself as yourself without the need to feel better than someone else. It is easy to feel big when someone else fails where you *have* made it. That is one side of envy. The other is the need to tear other people down to your own size. All of us have such needs. They are basic to our nature. That is why one of the ten most urgent things God has to tell Israel concerns envy.

Yet that same standard—namely, if God had ten commandments to give, what makes these the ten most important ones—may serve us, too. These are the ten basic things because they cover our relationships to God, to the world, and to other people. If people followed these laws, the world would be the way the prophets imagined it could be.

Only Ten?

At the same time, you surely can discover ten commandments for other important parts of your own life. You can think of ten mitzvot to cover life in school or on the sports field or in relations among boys and girls. If you do make such a list, you are apt to find that your ten commandments fit very nicely within one or more of God's list of ten things. The strength of the Ten Commandments is that they can lead to many times ten commandments.

We have been brief in dealing with them here. That is because, unlike the Shema, the Ten Commandments speak for themselves. They are easy to get at. And, also, the Ten Commandments cover so many parts of our life that it is easy to apply them and take them with us—even when we leave class and finish this book.

What If You Fail Even With These Ten?

Yet there is one open question: What if you can't keep the Ten Commandments (or any of the other mitzvot)? Are some more important than others? That question, you remember, troubled the prophets and the rabbis of old. They kept looking for 613 or 11 or 3 or 1. The Shema stands for the one among many, to love God with all your heart, soul, and might. In the same way, Hillel says the one among many is to love your neighbor as yourself. Even at our weakest, these are commandments we must seek to preserve.

Now we again must ask, what lies at the bottom of it all? What is the main point in the multitude of matters of do and don't, feel, think, be this, be that? It is the next to the last question regarding the mitzvot. It is, furthermore, the question facing you as a bar or bat mitzvah. What is it all about? What am I all about?

The mark of someone ready to become a bat mitzvah or bar mitzvah is the readiness to ask that question. When you begin to wonder about yourself and why you are here and what you can be and will be, you *are* at the age of mitzvot. What happens in the family and the synagogue simply confirms what is already true inside you. The way you live following your bar or bat mitzvah is your answer to "What am I all about?"

That brings us back to your making choices. When you become a bar or bat mitzvah, you take on the "yoke of the commandments," and the Ten Commandments, above all, become your responsibility. To reach the age of the commandments is to become responsible to do, at the very least, these ten things. It also means to have the choice of doing or not doing them, to accept or reject the yoke, to become or not become Israel, the Jewish people, within yourself. So far as you really do make these choices, you must make the momentous decision to define yourself within these mitzvot above all. How do you know whether or not you wish to do so?

Why Choose to Be Commanded?

The answer must be to ask, What sort of person do I want to be? The meaning of the Ten Commandments is then clear. A person who keeps the Ten Commandments does not steal, lie, abuse or misuse someone else, envy others. A person who keeps the Ten Commandments does worship God, has a day of rest, honors and respects parents. A person who does not keep the Ten Commandments is free to steal, lie, cheat, abuse, misuse, despise, hate. To become a person responsible to keep the mitzvot is to face that choice—and many other choices like it. It is to decide what sort of person you wish to be, and then to accept the disciplines that will shape you into that person. We are what we do: the commandments are what we are supposed to do so that we may become what we wish ourselves to be.

LOOKING BACK, LOOKING FORWARD

The Ten Commandments themselves are the main points of this chapter. The open question is the one of ourselves, for we are weak and frail. We make promises that we cannot keep. We hope for things we cannot be. None of us live totally the way we feel about life on the day on which we celebrate reaching the age of mitzvot. How you feel as you stand before the community as a bat or bar mitzvah may not be how you feel the next day or the next week. To put it more poetically: we climb mountains, but we do not live on them.

Now we must ask what happens when we cannot keep all of the mitzvot all of the time.

TO LIVE BY THE MITZVOT

Life might seem easier if the mitzvot provided the right answers for every choice we have to make. But as we face choices in life, the commandments almost seem to make these choices more complicated. There may even come times when you will have to choose to set aside a commandment or break it for the sake of something more important, as we shall see.

Yet there are three commandments that you must always keep, no matter what, even if you have to die to keep them. You must not worship any gods but God. You must not murder. You must not have sexual relations with people in your near family.

And there is one thing further: If you are in a public place and someone tries to force you to deny God by causing you to do some unimportant thing the commandments say you must not do, or by not doing some minor thing the commandments say you must do, then you must show that God is holy by honoring even that unimportant or minor mitzvah.

There are Ten Commandments. There is the great commandment to love God. There is the commandment to study Torah. There are the 613 commandments. But all of these now turn to you. When you are in a real-life situation, you must make your own judgments. At that moment, your moment of decision, you will find guidance in this teaching. You will want to remember it well.

When Rules are Set Aside

This teaching from the Tosefta, a commentary of the rabbis which helps explain the Mishnah, begins with a situation. The situation comes from the Bible. A thief is breaking and entering. Someone hears the noise the thief is making, strikes the thief and kills him. Is the person who killed the thief guilty of murder? The Bible says no.

But, the Bible continues, if the sun is out, if it is daytime, and the thief can be seen clearly, then the person killing him *is* guilty of murder.

The rabbis (Rabbi Aha, who is remembering this teaching of Rabbi Akiba) know that killing is always a crime. So how can the Bible say that if a thief is killed at night, no one shall be guilty? And, what difference does it make if it is at night or in the day?

The key to the puzzle is the one moment in which taking a life is permitted—when it is done to save another life. So, the person killing the thief at night does so because there is danger that the thief is about to kill the people in the house. But, if it is daytime, then the thief can be seen and watched. There is no need to kill the thief until we know for certain that there is danger to the people in the house.

In the first case, killing the thief at night, a commandment—You shall not kill—is set aside for a special case. Even though there is doubt as to whether or not the thief is a danger to the life of the people in the house, it is night and observing the thief further is difficult. One suspects the worst; one must act as if the worst were about to happen—as if a life were about to be taken.

That teaches us something about mitzvot in general. Let's see how it is worked out in the teaching before us:

> *Rabbi Aha says in the name of Rabbi Akiba, It is written in Scriptures*, If a thief be found breaking in and is struck so that he dies, no one shall be held guilty of it; but if the sun has risen upon him, someone shall be held guilty.
>
> *Now the [safety of] the householder—is it a matter of certainty or a matter of doubt? You must say that it is a matter of doubt [since we do not know for certain that the thief will kill the householder].*
>
> *Now if they kill one person to save the life of another which is subject only to doubt as to its safety, is it not logical that they should set aside the rules of the*

Sabbath in order to save a life which is in doubt [as to its safety].

See, the mitzvot were given to Israel so that they may live by them, since it says, You shall therefore keep My statutes and My ordinances, by doing which a person shall live—*to live by them; not to die by them.*

Nothing in the whole world is more important than [saving a life when there is] a threat to life—except for idolatry, incest, and murder. Of what times are we speaking here? Of [normal times] when there is no persecution.

But in a time of persecution, for even the slightest of the lesser commandments, a person must give up his life, since it says, And you shall not profane My holy name, but I will be hallowed among the people of Israel, *and it says,* The Lord has made everything for its purpose [*and even the slightest of the commandments has its purpose in a time of persecution*].

The Three Demands

Three things are demanded. First, that life be held more important than mitzvot. The commandments are given to Israel only so Israel, the Jewish people, will live by them.

Second, there are three commandments that may never be violated under any circumstances.

Third, in a time of persecution—which for us is a time when social pressures threaten to destroy our way of life—no commandment is trivial. We may have to give our all for even the most minor thing.

This third point is most essential to a bar mitzvah or a bat mitzvah, because even now there are many pressures against your taking to heart the new position in the community you are reaching. These pressures often come from other Jews, not from unfriendly non-Jews. If you are faithful to the mitzvot, you may cause other Jews, who are not faithful to them, to feel guilty. They may feel they are not as good as you. You must not do or say anything to lead them to that feeling. Still, they may come to it on their own.

Often, they will not admire or look up to you. Instead, they will put pressure on you to be like them. In the Jewish community, the Jew faithful to the mitzvot may sometimes feel among non-Jews for, after all, everyone knows that a great many Jews in our times are not faithful to the mitzvot. Whether that means they do not keep the laws regarding holy days and the Sabbath, or whether it means they do not study Torah, or whether it means that the teachings about how people should treat one another are foreign to them, hardly matters. Whatever mitzvah you name, many Jews do not keep it. So being a true bat mitzvah or bar mitzvah may mean that within the Jewish community you are as separate and set apart as Jews are within the non-Jewish community. So be it.

With this in mind, let us unpack the teaching to see how the three demands are made and what each one means to us.

1. To Live By Them

The first demand is that mitzvot be a part of life. Mitzvot are not to be more important than life, they come to make our lives richer. This is an important statement. It is very straightforward. It means that if you have a choice of saving a life or doing a mitzvah, you save the life. If, in order to save another human life, you have to do something on the Sabbath that you would not ordinarily do, it becomes a mitzvah to break the rules of the Sabbath and to save the life.

Now you may say, "Of course. That makes sense." Yet there are people who forget and think of the mitzvot as goals, rather than rules for reaching goals—as the prophets and rabbis teach. For some people, doing the mitzvah exactly the right way is more important than why you do the mitzvah, or what the mitzvah is supposed to mean. When people think this way, they turn the mitzvot into mere routines or habits. (In some ways, it is true, the mitzvot should become natural and normal; and comfortable, like a friendly routine.) But when the mitzvot become an iron track that controls your life, when you no longer make decisions and through doing mitzvot aim to make your life holy—then the mitzvot no longer improve your life. They control it. They rule you. Just as if you were subject to a terrible habit you could not control, such as smoking, so with the mitzvot. You can turn them from a way of living to a set of habits.

When the rabbis tell us that we must regard the mitzvah of saving a life as paramount, they mean one simple thing. No mitzvah may stand in the way of saving someone's life. You may not have the good fortune of saving someone's life many times. Yet there are ways in which the mitzvot can be turned from life-saving and life-enriching to life-deadening. They can make life dreary if they become matters of habit rather than occasions for choice. If you do mitzvot automatically, never thinking of what they mean, you can become a robot, someone who does not make decisions at all. That is not what mitzvot are for.

So, we are told that the mitzvot are given to help us live. And, since we are free to choose, the mitzvot themselves have the right to be vital and alive before us: things we find surprising, important, worthy of thinking about. That is not to say that every time you keep the Sabbath you have to decide in advance that this week you will keep the Sabbath. It is to say that some time when you keep the Sabbath you must remember that you do so because you choose to accept the "yoke of the commandments," to do God's will by keeping the Sabbath. If the Sabbath is only a habit, it is not holy. If it is only a matter of choice, it is not a mitzvah. You must walk a path between these two points of danger.

2. Except for Idolatry, Incest, and Murder

There are three mitzvot about what one must never do, under any circumstances, at any time. To avoid breaking these negative commandments, you have to give your life. Period.

They are these three: (a) Not to commit idolatry; (b) not to have sexual relations with someone of your near family; (c) not to commit murder.

Clearly, as you approach the age of being subject to mitzvot, you cannot imagine doing any of those things. Yet you have to know that they are principal and must never be done. You must know because you may think of things you might do, or could do, that fall into the same category—even if they seem less, if they seem way down the line.

For example, you would not actually murder another person. But you can make someone else wish he or she were dead. You are not likely to have sexual relations with close relatives. More obviously, you are not likely to "worship idols," whatever that can mean in this day and age. But you can very well turn something into an object of worship. For an object of worship is something you pine for, demand, live for. Obviously, nice clothes are not an idol. But when nice clothes are all that matter to you, . . . then the picture is clear.

Even as we try to see how these harsh words can be made simpler and closer, we must not tame them. We must not treat them as if they were talking only about the small and obvious things we can find in our own everyday world. When the ancient rabbis speak of murder, idolatry, and incest, they mean just that, and they mean to say that our people, as much as any other, is fully capable of the worst kinds of behavior. That is why we need the mitzvot—to purify our hearts, to tell us what we must never do under any circumstances, at any time, and for any reason.

3. In Times of Persecution

Now comes a third demand. No mitzvah is unimportant if someone else makes it important. That idea is taught in harsh and unyielding terms. When Jews are under pressure to give up or violate the mitzvot, then any mitzvah becomes crucial. Building a *sukkah*, for instance, becomes as important as not murdering. There comes a time when the Jew must defy the world, even in the most trivial and unimportant way. That time comes when the world says to the Jew, "Give up your Torah by doing this small thing." The small thing may be so unimportant that you never in your life gave thought to it. But at that moment it is the most important mitzvah in the world. If need be, at all costs, you must do that mitzvah, if it is a deed, or you must carry out the mitzvah not to do that thing, if the mitzvah is phrased in the negative.

The Courage to Be Different

Don't think it is easy to be a Jew, a bat mitzvah or bar mitzvah. It is not easy. It is hard and it takes courage. First, many people don't like Jews. There is little we can do about it. We are not like other people, because we are Jews. So long as we are different in the ways in which we are different, there will be people who will not like us. It is easy, almost natural, to dislike what seems different or strange. We ourselves know those feelings toward others. Today, as you already know, perhaps a third of all Americans have uncomplimentary opinions of Jews in general

The Teaching

ר׳ אַחָא אָמַר מִשֵׁם ר׳
עֲקִיבָא הֲרֵי הוּא אוֹמֵר אִם
בַּמַחְתֶּרֶת יִמָּצֵא הַגַּנָּב וגו׳,

בַּעַל הַבַּיִת מָהוּ וַדַּיי אוֹ
סָפֵק, הֱוֵי אוֹמֵר סָפֵק,
אִם הוֹרְגִין נֶפֶשׁ לְהַחֲיוֹת

נֶפֶשׁ בְּסָפֵק, דִּין הוּא
שֶׁיְּדַחוּ אֶת הַשַּׁבָּת לְהַחֲיוֹת
נֶפֶשׁ בְּסָפֵק,

Rabbi Aha says in the name of Rabbi Akiba, It is written in Scriptures, *If a thief be found breaking in and is struck so that he dies, no one shall be held guilty of it; but if the sun has risen upon him, someone shall be held guilty* (Exodus 22:1–2).

Now the [safety of] the householder—is it a matter of certainty or a matter of doubt? You must say that it is a matter of doubt [since we do not know for certain that the thief will kill the householder].

Now if they kill one person to save the life of another which is subject only to doubt as to its safety, is it not logical that they should set aside the rules of the Sabbath in order to save a life which is in doubt [as to its safety].

From the Tosefta: Shabbat 15:17

הָא לֹא נָתְנוּ מִצְוֹת
לְיִשְׂרָאֵל אֶלָּא לִחְיוֹת בָּהֶן,
שֶׁנֶּאֱמַר אֲשֶׁר יַעֲשֶׂה אוֹתָם
הָאָדָם וָחַי בָּהֶם, וָחַי בָּהֶן
וְלֹא שֶׁיָּמוּת בָּהֶן.

אֵין כָּל דָּבָר עוֹמֵד בִּפְנֵי
פִּקּוּחַ נֶפֶשׁ, חוּץ מֵע״ז
וְגִלּוּי עֲרָיוֹת וּשְׁפִיכוּת
דָּמִים. בְּמִי דְּבָרִים אֲמוּרִים
שֶׁלֹּא בִּשְׁעַת הַשְּׁמָד,

אֲבָל בִּשְׁעַת הַשְּׁמָד
אֲפִילוּ מִצְוָה קַלָּה
שֶׁבְּקַלּוֹת אָדָם נוֹתֵן נַפְשׁוֹ
עָלֶיהָ, שֶׁנֶּאֱמַר וְלֹא תְחַלְּלוּ
אֶת שֵׁם קָדְשִׁי וְגוֹ׳ וְאוֹמֵר
כֹּל פָּעַל ה׳ לַמַּעֲנֵהוּ.

See, the mitzvot were given to Israel so that they may live by them, since it says, *You shall therefore keep My statutes and My ordinances, by doing which a person shall live* (Leviticus 18:5)—to live by them; not to die by them.

Nothing in the whole world is more important than [saving a life when there is] a threat to life—except for idolatry, incest, and murder. Of what times are we speaking here? Of [normal times] when there is no persecution.

But in a time of persecution, for even the slightest of the lesser commandments, a person must give up his life, since it says, *And you shall not profane My holy name, but I will be hallowed among the people of Israel* (Leviticus 22:32), and it says, *The Lord has made everything for its purpose* (Proverbs 16:4) [and even the slightest of the commandments has its purpose in a time of persecution].

and apply them to Jews they meet. Often it is necessary to show you are a Jew by keeping the mitzvot. In fact, it is usually not clear from how you live that you are a Jew. So don't think persecution is something that happens somewhere else, or in times long gone—anywhere but here and now. The contrary is the case. The pressure to conform is always there.

Also, to keep the mitzvot—whether they are commandments about how we deal with one another or commandments regarding our feelings and dealings with God—makes us different all the time. If you keep the Sabbath, you know that you cannot go to school dances on Friday nights. If you keep the dietary laws, you know that you have to make choices about what you eat. If you keep Passover, you will not eat bread when others do. If you study Torah, you will be changed—you will no longer be like other people. These are facts of a Jewish life.

True, there are no mobs in our streets crying for Jewish blood. But there is a constant pressure on all of us to conform, to be like everyone else. So far as Jews are different, they resist that pressure. So long as the Jews form a group, they are separate from other people. So when the rabbis say that there comes a time when Jews must defy the world, that time is not for a moment in some unfortunate place. That time is every day; that place is wherever you are.

What Do You Live For? What Do You Live By?

These three demands pose a question for you. As you reach the age of the commandments, you have to ask yourself, What are the most important things in your life? The passage we have studied is a way of stating that issue: What do you really live for?

If you want to know what someone really prizes, ask what that person lives for. Some people want to be famous, to have everyone know who they are. Some people want to be smart, to know everything about everything. Some want to paint great pictures or make great music. There are many things people hope for themselves. What Israel, the Jewish people, hopes for we already know. The prayer Ahavah Rabbah has told us. The Shema has let us know. The Ten Commandments spell it out.

Yet it is one thing to hope for high achievement. It is another to live an everyday life. Most people settle for much less than their hopes. As you become a bat mitzvah or a bar mitzvah, you make yourself large promises. You think long thoughts. You feel, as you grow to maturity in body and in mind, you can do just about anything you want. This is a happy time. It is easy to make promises. Dreaming costs nothing.

But it is hard to keep promises. A dream that does not come true may become a nightmare. Life is disappointing for most people much of the time. It is not because of what happens out there, in a world that does not see someone's true value. It is because of what happens in here—in your own heart.

People spend much time feeling sorry for themselves. Others seem to be better than they are—better at sports, better at making friends, better at schoolwork, better at making decisions and sticking to them. So the moment of celebrating a bat mitzvah or a bar mitzvah may lead to hopes that will never come true, promises that are never to be kept. After all, how many boys and girls pass bar mitzvah and bat mitzvah and never again walk into a Jewish schoolroom or into a synagogue for services?

The mitzvot are like these promises. They describe a beautiful world. If you do everything they say, or do not do what they tell you not to do, you will be a truly noble person. You will help make a wonderful world. But the mitzvot are few and our impulses and desires are many. The mitzvot are meant to purify us. But we are what we are—less than angels, more than animals. So the long lists of dos and don'ts lay out a splendid vision of ourselves. It is a vision worth imagining. But we also have to reckon with our own reality. We are great to dream dreams. And we are less than our dreams.

If I Can't Do Them All, Shall I Give Up?

We need not give it all up and say we are not worthy of the mitzvot. We do not, we cannot say: Because I cannot keep them all, I shall do none of them. We are not perfect. We are flesh and blood, ordinary people. So we have to measure ourselves by what we can do. You may not be as tall as you want to be. Still, you matter, no matter how tall you are. You may admire other people's physical or mental gifts. Yet you are what you are, you should appreciate and enjoy yourself. You have only one life, one body, one mind. The choice is not to imagine being someone else. The choice is you or nothing.

The rabbis of the Talmud understand that fact. They realize that the mitzvot represent a high ideal. They know that people cannot always do everything. They make the point that if you cannot do everything, you can and must do some things. And the rabbis speak of those things that one must do under all circumstances and at all costs. They are very specific; and there are only three things.

Now at this point you must wonder what has happened to the 613 commandments that become one; or to the great commandment to love God; or to the commandment that Hillel pointed to, to love your neighbor as yourself; or to what Yohanan ben Zakkai said about how we were created to study Torah. All of this is very noble and beautiful. But in the crunch it will not help you much. What will help you are the basic principles of the law of Judaism.

Being Different, Being Yourself, Being Israel

In the end, keeping the mitzvot means being different. Standing up against the world is not such a bad thing. It means making choices rather than letting other people choose for you. It means discovering who you are through everyday acts of courage. It means being different when it might be easier to conform and be like others. For you it may mean not following the crowd when it comes to sex, drugs, liquor. It surely means sticking to your own ideals, to the best that you want for yourself.

Defying the world in these ways is a good thing. It is why you are becoming a bar or a bat mitzvah. For if the Jewish people had not defied the world for all of its history, you would not be what you are today. To be a Jew is to stand against the majority.

We are a small people. We have few friends or allies in the world. Our way of life, the Torah, makes us different from other people. To remain ourselves we cannot become like others. So if you become a true bar mitzvah or bat mitzvah, you become another link in a very strong chain that goes back to the beginnings of Israel at Sinai and goes forward to the end of time.

LOOKING BACK, LOOKING FORWARD

These are the main points of this chapter: (1) There are three commandments you must keep at all costs; (2) But the purpose of the commandments is so that we may live. (3) The only things we must truly be prepared to die for are not to commit idolatry, not to have sexual relations with near of kin, and not to murder. (4) In a time of persecution, every commandment is equally a way to sanctify God's name in the world. (5) So there are many times in which to be a Jew, to sanctify God's name in the world, we have to be different from other people. We have to defy the world.

Only one question remains to be answered for a person reaching the age of commandments: Why bother? What good is it all to the Jews in general, and to me in particular? The mitzvot lay heavy demands upon me. They say how I must feel and what I must do and not do. What happens to me if I don't keep the commandments, and what rewards are there for keeping them?

WHAT'S IN IT FOR ISRAEL? WHAT'S IN IT FOR ME?

You cannot ask, what's in it for me alone? You always are a Jew, no matter what you do or do not do, no matter whether you do good or bad things. So you must ask, What's in it for Israel, the Jewish people? But you are a part of Israel, so you have a right to know what your share will be.

The answer comes in a single word: holy. The commandments make us holy. To be holy is to be set apart by God for the service of God. (It does not mean to be holier than someone else. It means to be holy and that is all.) The word that always is said when a commandment or a mitzvah is at hand is *kadosh*.

In this chapter we will discuss three separate texts. Each makes a point that we must understand if we are to understand everything that came before this. Begin by reading all three of them.

> *(1) Blessed are You, O Lord our God, Ruler of the universe, who has made us holy by Your commandments, and commanded us to light the Sabbath candle.*

> *(2) Rabbi Hananiah ben Akashya says, The Holy One, blessed is he, wished to give merit to Israel; therefore he multiplied for them the Torah and the commandments, as it says, It pleased the Lord for his righteousness' sake to magnify the Law and glorify it.*

> *(3) Ben Azzai says, Run to do a lesser mitzvah as quickly as you run to do an important one—and flee from sin; for one mitzvah leads to another mitzvah just as one sin leads to another sin; for the reward for a mitzvah is another mitzvah, and the payment for a sin is another sin.*

Israel and Me

You are not all by youself when you become a bat mitzvah or a bar mitzvah. You are a part of Israel, the Jewish people. You share the fate and destiny of Israel wherever they are; and all Israel is part of you and shares your fate and destiny. So you cannot ask, Why should I, in particular, do this mitzvah or not do what the mitzvah warns against? You can only ask, Why should we, Israel, do these things and refrain from doing those things? You were born to be Israel and you will die Israel; and nothing you do, or do not do, in your entire life, will make you any less, or any more, Israel than you are on the day you reach the age of the commandments.

We are what we are, but always we are Israel, the Jewish people. Together, we have no choice. Individuals may have a choice. They may choose to go off and try to be something other than Israel. But the people of Israel will always be there, always remind the world that Israel lives on. So, if you want to know, What's in it for me? you ask a perfectly natural and normal question. But you ask in vain. For in the setting of the life of Torah, of Israel, of mitzvot, there is no choice, to be or not to be. We are what we are, because the Torah says that is what we are. In the same way, Israel, the Jewish people, cannot ask, What is in it for us? Israel is what it is. There is no chance to ask, to be or not to be? These are the facts of life, as much as breathing is a fact of life, as much as being the son or daughter of our mothers and our fathers is a fact of life.

What Kind of Jew?

The choice comes then: What kind of Israel, what kind of Jew? There the choice is wholly in the hands of each of us, and it is entirely in the hands of the Jewish people all together. The purpose of the commandments in answering the question What kind of Israel? is very clear.

We speak of it each time we do one of the commandments that requires a blessing. For, as you must know, when we do a deed and wish the deed to be a mitzvah, we recite a blessing before it. And the blessing contains the whole answer to the question we now raise.

Who Has Made Us Holy Through Your Commandments

You light a candle. It is on a birthday cake. You sing, "Happy birthday." The candle is blown out. Someone is made happy.

There is no electricity. You light a candle. You now have a light. You can go about your business.

It is Friday. The sun is setting. You light a candle. You say a blessing. You have welcomed the Sabbath day.

What blessing do you say to accomplish this miracle? How have you changed what is ordinary and everyday into what is holy? This is the blessing:

> *Blessed are You, O Lord our God, Ruler of the universe,*
> *who has made us holy by Your commandments, and*
> *commanded us to light the Sabbath candle.*

You can seek the answer to our question, What kind of Israel? in this set of words we say every time we do a mitzvah of this kind: " . . . who has made us holy by Your commandments, and commanded us . . . " What the mitzvot do is make us holy. We are made holy by being commanded.

The Teaching
From the Prayer Book

בָּרוּךְ אַתָּה, יְיָ אֱלֹהֵינוּ,
מֶלֶךְ הָעוֹלָם, אֲשֶׁר קִדְּשָׁנוּ
בְּמִצְוֹתָיו וְצִוָּנוּ לְהַדְלִיק נֵר
שֶׁל שַׁבָּת.

Blessed are You, O Lord our God, Ruler of the universe, who has made us holy by Your commandments, and commanded us to light the Sabbath candle.

Holy

What does it mean to be made holy?

Holy means two things. It means being different. And it means being different for God's sake. When we say Israel is made holy, we are made holy, we are saying both of these things. First, we mean that we are made different by the mitzvot, by doing this mitzvah in particular; and, second, we are made different in the way in which God wants us to be different.

The first is a simple fact. Only Israel lights a candle to welcome the Sabbath. Since only Israel does this commandment, Israel is made holy—meaning, different—from everyone else, just as Sabbath is different from the six working days.

The second statement is not so obvious. God commands us to do the mitzvot in general, and this mitzvah in particular. So we are commanded to light this candle in a way in which we are not commanded to light a candle for a birthday cake. We celebrate a birthday in this way out of affection or delight. We light the Sabbath candle because we must. The act is the same in both cases. The attitude changes everything, we remember. We do this because God wants us to do it. It makes us holy, meaning different. It makes us holy, meaning it makes us what God wants us to be. We do at that moment, in that action, what God wants us to do.

How are We Jews Made Holy?

Israel is made holy by the commandments. What's in it for Israel, the Jewish people, then, is holiness—being a holy people and serving the holy God. Why us? Why holiness? Not because we are better than anyone else; not because, in ourselves, we are more holy than anyone else. We certainly are not more numerous. We cannot claim to be smarter or nicer or more worthy. God loves us, as God loves all peoples everywhere. God shows love to us by telling us how to live, by giving us Torah and mitzvot. How God shows love to other peoples is not for us to say, or even know. But how God loves us and what God wants of us in particular we can say and we do know, because we have the Torah and because we are commanded to do the mitzvot.

This is how an ancient rabbi states our point:

Rabbi Hananiah ben Akashya says, The Holy One, blessed is he, wished to give merit to Israel; therefore he multiplied for them the Torah and the commandments, as it says, It pleased the Lord for his righteousness' sake to magnify the Law and glorify it.

If you had to add up all the pluses and minuses of being Israel, the Jewish people, you might have to reckon with this statement of Rabbi Hananiah at the top of your list. Because God wished to give merit to Israel, God gave us a vast Torah and many mitzvot. This is how God shows love. That should not be surprising to you, since you have seen the same idea in Ahavah Rabbah. Nor is the idea that at the head of all the commandments stands the will and worth of God, for you noticed in the Ten Commandments that the first commandment is no commandment at all. It is the simple statement, "I am the Lord your God who brought you out of the land of Egypt, out of the house of bondage." Hananiah says simply and clearly what many of the great teachings we have studied already tell us. The mitzvah is an act of love. God loves us, so God gives us mitzvot. We love God, so we carry out the mitzvot, because we are commanded to do so.

Long ago, we compared this love of God for Israel to the love our parents, our mother or our father, show when they make demands of us. Your celebration of your

The Teaching

From the Mishnah: Makkot 3:16

רַבִּי חֲנַנְיָה בֶּן עֲקַשְׁיָא
אוֹמֵר: רָצָה הַקָּדוֹשׁ בָּרוּךְ
הוּא לְזַכּוֹת אֶת יִשְׂרָאֵל,
לְפִיכָךְ הִרְבָּה לָהֶם תּוֹרָה
וּמִצְווֹת, שֶׁנֶּאֱמַר. ה׳ חָפֵץ
לְמַעַן צִדְקוֹ יַגְדִּיל תּוֹרָה
וְיַאְדִּיר.

Rabbi Hananiah ben Akashya says, The Holy One, blessed is he, wished to give merit to Israel; therefore he multiplied for them the Torah and the commandments, as it says, *It pleased the Lord for his righteousness' sake to magnify the Law and glorify it* (Isaiah 42:21).

bar or bat mitzvah is part of this world of love—your father's and your mother's love for you, God's love for Israel. Just as God celebrates Israel, so your family celebrates you. Just as God gives Torah and mitzvot to Israel, your family gives you many lessons and much responsibility. You may say, I'd rather not have the lessons and the responsibility. But, then, would you not want the love, the caring? Would you give up the knowledge that people think you matter and what you do matters? It is the difference between being nobody and nothing, or being somebody to many people. To be commanded is to say that someone cares what you do so much as to tell you what to do. To be subject to mitzvot, to be responsible to carry out mitzvot, is to say that God cares so much for you as to want you to live a good and holy life.

The Reward of Doing a Mitzvah

What is in it for you? To do a mitzvah has only one result: to do yet another. What is your reward? A mitzvah's reward is the mitzvah, the knowledge that you have carried out what God wants you to do, and you can do it yet again and again. Again, the obvious examples are the chessplayer, the writer, the doctor, the lawyer, the athlete, the artist, the musician, the scientist, the mathematician. The more we work at what we do, the better we are at it—the reward of doing well is doing well again, or doing even better. That is the core of what Ben Azzai taught.

> *Ben Azzai says, Run to do a lesser mitzvah as quickly as you run to do an important one—and flee from sin; for one mitzvah leads to another mitzvah just as one sin leads to another sin; for the reward for a mitzvah is another mitzvah, and the payment for a sin is another sin.*

If the truth be told, what Ben Azzai says is that you are entering a world in which what you do is its own reward. What you are is what you must continue to be. Israel is Israel, because that is what Israel must be. You are what you are—you are a Jew. Because God loves Israel, God gives us Torah and mitzvot. The reward of mitzvot is to do mitzvot. The purpose of it all is to make us holy: " . . . who has made us holy by Your commandments, and commanded us . . . "

The Teaching

From the Mishnah: Avot 4:2

בֶּן עַזַּאי אוֹמֵר: הֱוֵי רָץ לְמִצְוָה קַלָּה כְּבַחֲמוּרָה, וּבוֹרֵחַ מִן הָעֲבֵרָה; שֶׁמִּצְוָה גּוֹרֶרֶת מִצְוָה וַעֲבֵרָה גּוֹרֶרֶת עֲבֵרָה, שֶׁשְּׂכַר מִצְוָה מִצְוָה וּשְׂכַר עֲבֵרָה עֲבֵרָה.

Ben Azzai says, Run to do a lesser mitzvah as quickly as you run to do an important one—and flee from sin; for one mitzvah leads to another mitzvah just as one sin leads to another sin; for the reward for a mitzvah is another mitzvah, and the payment for a sin is another sin.

What I have described is a world—complete, whole, enduring. It is a world of good people, trying to carry out the mitzvot that cause them to be different, defying a world that wants them to be the same as all others—which means, wants them not to be at all.

To Stand in a Circle

What I have described is the journey to that world, the way you get there. To put it another way: To be Israel, to be subject to the mitzvot, is to stand within a circle—to be inside a world where everything fits together with everything else. But how do you step into this circle? How do you find your way into this whole and complete world of Israel, the Jewish people?

If you were born Jewish, you are born into that world. You face the question of how to form yourself into the Israel that you were born to be.

If you were not born Jewish but wish to be Israel, part of the Jewish people, the question is not much different. You also have to form yourself into the Israel that you now choose to be.

In either case, coming to the age of bat or bar mitzvah, you now celebrate the occasion of reaching a stage of maturity marked by changes in your outlook and in your body. This is a time of new beginnings, of a new place in life. It can also be a time of new beginnings in that world of mitzvot and Torah. The occasion of the bar or bat mitzvah celebration places you squarely within the circle of Torah and mitzvah. You do not have to wonder how to find your way within a world in which everything fits together with everything else. When you reach the age of the mitzvot, you enter the realm marked out by mitzvot and by Torah, by life within the community of Israel. You become responsible, and you may become holy—a part of the holiness made possible for Israel by the commandments: " . . . who has made us holy by Your commandments, and commanded us . . . "

LOOKING BACK, LOOKING FORWARD

These are the main points in this chapter: (1) We always are Israel, no matter what we do or do not do. (2) The question is not whether, but what kind. What kind of person to be. What kind of Israel to be. (3) The kind of Jew we can be is the kind produced by the commandments—one made holy. (4) God wants Israel to bring merit to our lives; therefore, God gives us mitzvot, through which Israel receives God's love and expresses love to God.

(5) The reward of doing a mitzvah is doing another mitzvah.